German Field Fortifications 1939–45

Gordon L Rottman · Illustrated by Ian Palmer

Series editors Marcus Cowper and Nikolai Bogdanovic

First published in Great Britain in 2004 by Osprey Publishing, Elms Court,
Chapel Way, Botley, Oxford OX2 9LP, United Kingdom.
Email: info@ospreypublishing.com

© 2004 Osprey Publishing Ltd.

ISBN 1 84176 761 1

Editorial by Ilios Publishing, Oxford, UK (www.iliospublishing.com)
Cartography by Map Studio, Romsey, Hants
Design: Ken Vail Graphic Design, Cambridge, UK
Index by Alison Worthington
Originated by The Electronic Page Company, Cwmbran, UK
Printed and bound by L-Rex Printing Company Ltd

04 05 06 07 08   10 9 8 7 6 5 4 3 2 1

A CIP catalogue record for this book is available from the British Library.

FOR A CATALOGUE OF ALL BOOKS PUBLISHED BY OSPREY MILITARY AND AVIATION
PLEASE CONTACT:

Osprey Direct UK, PO Box 140, Wellingborough,
Northants, NN8 2FA, United Kingdom.
Email: info@ospreydirect.co.uk

Osprey Direct USA, c/o MBI Publishing, PO Box 1,
729 Prospect Ave, Osceola, WI 54020, USA.
Email: info@ospreydirectusa.com

www.ospreypublishing.com

Image credits

Measurements

Distances, ranges and dimensions are given in metric values in this
volume:

1 millimetre (mm)	0.0394 inches
1 centimetre (cm)	0.3937 inches
1 metre (m)	1.0936 yards
1 kilometre (km)	0.6214 miles
1 kilogram (kg)	2.2046 pounds
1 tonne (t)	0.9842 long ton (UK)

The Fortress Study Group (FSG)

The object of the FSG is to advance the education of the public in
the study of all aspects of fortifications and their armaments,
especially works constructed to mount or resist artillery. The FSG
holds an annual conference in September over a long weekend
with visits and evening lectures, an annual tour abroad lasting
about eight days, and an annual Members' Day.

The FSG journal *FORT* is published annually, and its newsletter
Casemate is published three times a year. Membership is
international. For further details, please contact:

The Secretary, c/o 6 Lanark Place, London W9 1BS, UK

Contents

Introduction

While the German Army (*deutschen Heer*) is perhaps best known for elaborate, massive concrete and steel fortifications, such as the Westwall (or 'Siegfried Line') and Atlantikwall, the fortifications that a German soldier was most familiar with were the ones he dug himself. Whether built on the sprawling steppes of Russia, in the deserts of North Africa, in the mountains of Italy, in European hills and forests, or among the rubble of countless battered cities, these were the fortifications that truly defined the boundaries of the Third Reich.

The focus of this study is the field fortifications constructed by combat troops defending the frontline. Large, permanent fortifications are beyond the scope of this book, and are dealt with in accompanying Fortress titles (such as Fortress 15: *Germany's West Wall*). The core focus will be temporary and semi-permanent crew-served weapon positions and individual and small-unit fighting positions, built with local materials and occasionally construction *matériel*. Little engineer support was provided: pioneer troops may have provided advice, but the infantry mostly built these positions and obstacles. However, pioneer (*Pionier*) and construction (*Baupionier*) units and Organisation Todt civilian labourers did sometimes prepare defences behind the front for units to fall back to.

While wartime intelligence studies and reports provide detailed information on German field defences, only limited post-war study has been undertaken. This is largely due to their temporary nature, and the fact that little survives of them today. The Wehrmacht (consisting of the Heer, Luftwaffe and Kriegsmarine) used the same basic doctrine and manuals for positioning and construction purposes as did the Waffen-SS. With the exception of local improvisation, a factor common to all armies in the field, all branches of the German armed forces employed these field fortifications and obstacles.

What the Germans did not want to experience again – a machine-gun platoon on the Western Front, 1914. Watercooled 7.92mm MG.08 heavy machine guns were reissued to fortress machine-gun battalions late in World War II.

German tactical defence doctrine

'Elastic defence'

The experiences on the Western Front during World War I had a strong influence (both negative and positive) on post-war defence doctrine. The positive aspect of World War I to the Germans, from the doctrinal standpoint, was the development of what is informally known as the 'elastic defence' (*elastische Kampfverfahren*, literally 'elastic battle procedures'). By 1916 it had been realised that solid multi-layered trench systems and an unyielding defence, aimed at holding on to every metre of ground, were impractical. Massive six-day artillery barrages would shatter defences and the defenders. General of Infantry Erich Ludendorff endorsed a more in-depth defence. While still relying on continuous interconnected trench lines, the defences were subdivided into three zones: (1) combat outpost zone with minimal lookouts to warn of attacks and keep patrols from penetrating deeper; (2) 1,500–3,000m-deep main battle zone with complex trench systems concentrated on key terrain (rather than rigid lines covering all areas) intended to halt the attack; and (3) rear zone with artillery and reserves. While the battle zone still relied on trench lines, to establish the new defences the Germans actually withdrew (previously unheard of) in some sectors to more easily defended terrain, placed many of the trenches on reverse slopes to mask them from enemy observation and fire, and established strongpoints on key terrain. The establishment of the combat zone, supported by long-range artillery, disrupted Allied attacks. After fighting its way through the outpost zone the attack would often exhaust itself in the battle zone. Rather than attempting to halt the attack outright, penetration of the battle zone was accepted. The attack would become bogged down among the defences, battered by artillery fire and counter-attacks. This was first implemented in April 1917, and by war's end in November 1918 the defences were completely rearranged under this concept. It had proved itself, and was adopted by the post-war Reichsheer in 1921.

In spite of the much-vaunted blitzkrieg concept of mobile warfare, in 1940 only 10 per cent of the German Army's 138 divisions were motorised. The infantry division's 27 rifle companies walked, and most artillery and supply transport were horse drawn. The lack of mechanisation had a major impact on how the Germans conducted defensive operations.

Mobile warfare

There were negative influences too of the experiences on the Western Front. The horror, misery and prolonged stalemate of trench or positional warfare (*Stellungskrieg*) encouraged many, like Hans von Seeckt, to find another way to wage war. Some form of mobile offensive was preferred and defence was regarded as necessary only for local holding actions or a temporary situation until the initiative was regained and the offensive resumed.

The elastic defence was codified in the two-volume manual called *Führung und Gefecht der verbundenen Waffen* (Leadership and Combat of the Combined Arms), published in 1921/23. This codification managed a compromise between those who still

favoured the elastic defence (the old 'trench school') and those espousing a more mobile form of warfare. The manual stated that either form of warfare could be employed depending on the situation, but it clearly preferred the elastic defence, with improvements. These entailed more depth (both within each zone and in the distances between zones), and in fluid situations it called for a fourth zone forward of the three traditional ones. This was an 'advanced position' of light mobile units, infantry and artillery, which would disrupt the attack and force the enemy to deploy early into battle formation. The advance units would then withdraw and constitute part of the reserve. Anti-armour defence was addressed, but there were few effective anti-armour weapons at the time, being prohibited for the Reichsheer. This took the form of artillery concentrations and obstacles. The combat outpost zone would consist only of individual and infantry weapon positions not connected by trenches.

Such was the theory. In practice, Colonel General Hans von Seeckt, acting chief of staff, strongly discouraged any officer (with some being relieved of duty) from practising the elastic defence. Seeckt desired a mobile war of manoeuvre and shunned defence. Though Seeckt resigned in 1926, his successors continued to abide by his views, which remained in effect until the early 1930s. The practice of the elastic defence was permitted in exercises though. The rearmament of Germany in 1933 gradually saw the means become available to practise a highly evolved form of mobile warfare. This was by no means Army-wide, as the new *deutschen Heer* was still largely an infantry force relying on horse artillery and horse-drawn supply columns (4,000–6,000 horses per division). The infantry division's 27 rifle companies may have walked, but the division did possess a degree of mechanisation via truck transport for headquarters, signal, anti-armour and pioneer elements. Divisional reconnaissance battalions too were increasingly mechanised, receiving motorcycles and scout cars, though horses and bicycles were still relied on.

The new defence doctrine, laid out in *Truppenführung* (Troop Command) in 1933, allowed the four previous zones a greater use of anti-armour obstacles, minefields, anti-armour guns behind the main battle position, and tanks assembled in the rear zone to support counter-attacks. The use of armour as a mobile counter-attack and manoeuvre force was not fully appreciated at this time though, as German tanks had played no role in defeating Allied tank breakthroughs in World War I. They would be held in the rear to engage enemy tanks that had broken through and to destroy them piecemeal as they wandered through the rear zone. There was disagreement on the employment of anti-armour guns. While some might be attached to the advanced-position forces, most were to be positioned behind the main battle position to block tank breakthroughs. Others urged that they be positioned forward to pick off approaching enemy armour and break up the attack early. Individual infantrymen were to attack roaming tanks with anti-armour rifles and hand mines, which proved to be inadequate. As the blitzkrieg ('lightning war') concept developed, the German Army became so offensively orientated that anything appearing too defensive in nature was at risk of being minimised. (Anti-armour gun *Panzerabwehr* units were redesignated armour-hunting *Panzerjäger* units on 1 April 1940: anti-armour guns were still called *Panzerabwehrkanone* or *Pak.* for short.)

In the first two years of World War II German defensive doctrine was of secondary importance. Units did of course assume defensive postures locally as the operational situation required. General defensive situations for large formations

The German 'elastic defence' concept.

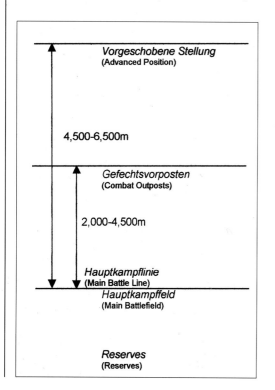

Vorgeschobene Stellung
(Advanced Position)

4,500–6,500m

Gefechtsvorposten
(Combat Outposts)

2,000–4,500m

Hauptkampflinie
(Main Battle Line)
Hauptkampffeld
(Main Battlefield)

Reserves
(Reserves)

The Eastern Front, 1942: a Panzer III, supported by Bf 110s, pushes into the Soviet Union. From early-1943 the Panzerwaffe no longer spearheaded the German Army, but largely acted as a mobile reserve to support the relied-on German defensive positions. (E. Gross)

were for the most part unnecessary. While units developed coastal defences, and the Afrikakorps was forced on the defensive at times, there was no major test of Germany's World War I elastic defence legacy. This would change in the winter of 1941. The broad expanses of the USSR, the necessity of defending on wide fronts, the decline in manpower, the loss of critical weapons and equipment, the massing of Soviet infantry, armour and artillery, and the terrain and weather themselves forced revisions in defensive doctrine. Other theatres of war, particularly North Africa and Italy, demanded additional changes and considerations. Eventually, soldiers fighting on different fronts would employ unique defensive tactics and adapt their fighting positions to local conditions.

The principles of unit defence

Regardless of the unique aspects of any given front, at all unit levels (defined by the Germans as regimental level and below) common principles for the establishment and conduct of defence were employed down to the squad.

Field fortifications were necessary during offensive movements too. Here infantrymen dig in for the night on a Russian steppe to provide protection to 7.5cm StuG III Ausf. F assault guns. These would be shallow slit trenches more suited to the role of a soldier's bed than a fighting position.

Space, distances, density of forces, and support would vary though, as would construction materials, types of fortifications, obstacles, and how they were deployed and manned.

High ground was always desirable for defensive positions for its observation advantages, extended fields of fire, and the fact that it is harder to fight uphill. In the desert even an elevation of a couple of metres would be an advantage. Natural terrain obstacles were integrated into the defence as much as possible. The routes and directions of possible enemy attacks were determined and infantry and supporting weapons were designated to cover these approaches. The goal was to destroy or disrupt the attackers by concentrating all available weapons before the enemy reached the main battle position. Effective employment of the different weapons organic to an infantry regiment was an art in itself, as each had capabilities and limitations: the weapons comprised light and heavy machine guns, anti-armour rifles, mortars, infantry guns, anti-armour guns, and supporting artillery to include anti-aircraft guns employed in a ground role.

A commander preparing a defence (and an attack) needed to identify the main effort point (*Schwerpunkt*). In attack, this was the point at which he would concentrate effort and firepower to break through the enemy defences. In defence, this was the point (assessed by the defending commander) where the enemy would attempt to break through: he would concentrate his defences and supporting weapons there. The defence would be established in depth, but not just using the four zones: each zone in itself would be organised in depth with the weapons providing mutual cover for each other. The employment of obstacles and minefields was critical, as it was fully understood that anti-armour weapons alone could not halt attacking tanks. Tank-hunting detachments with anti-armour rifles and hand mines were organised. In 1943 *Panzerfaust* and *Panzerschreck* shoulder-fired anti-armour rocket launchers began to replace these.

As the war progressed, anti-armour guns were increasingly employed in the main battle positions as well as in forward and outpost positions. Armoured

BELOW This squad battle trench (*Kampfgraben*) and approach trench (*Annäherungsgraben*) depicts the different positions incorporated into it: *Schützenloch für 2 Schützen* (rifle position for 2 riflemen), *Stichgräben* (slit trench), *Schützennischen* (fire steps), *M.G.-Feuerstellung* (machine-gun firing position), *Unterstand* (squad bunker), *Schützenausstieg* (exit ladder or steps), *Unterschlupf* (dugout). Note that the *feindwärts* arrow points in the direction of the enemy.

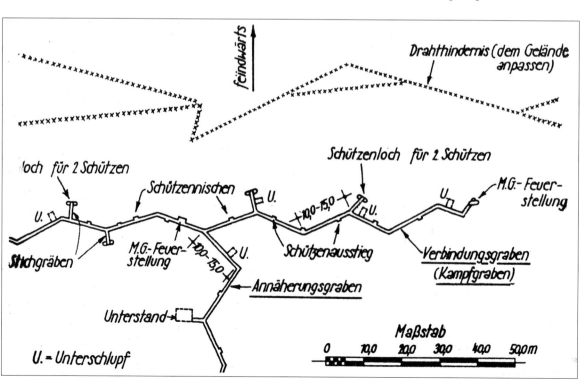

fighting vehicles (AFVs – tanks and assault guns) tended to be held as mobile reserves to counter-attack breakthroughs. There were many instances though where AFVs were employed as mobile pillboxes. As Germany lost ever more AFVs and infantry units were reduced in strength, the availability of mobile reserves dwindled. Rather than large units conducting major counter-attacks, they became increasingly localised and smaller, greatly reducing the German ability to regain lost ground.

Because of the extensive defensive frontages often required, 'strongpoint' defence was adopted on many fronts: there were no continuous frontlines. The gaps between mutually supporting strongpoints were extensive, to be covered by outposts, patrols and observation, backed up by long-range fire. This reduced the numbers of troops necessary to defend an area, but not necessarily the number of weapons. Strongpoints had to be well armed with the full range of weapons. Strong mobile reserves were a necessity. Still, the basic German doctrine of four defensive zones was retained to provide depth to the defence.

Camouflage efforts and all-round local security were continuous during the development of defensive positions. Camouflage had to prevent the enemy from detecting positions from the ground and the air. Reconnaissance forward of the defensive zones was essential to warn of the enemy's approach and his activities. The Germans developed a good capability of determining when and where the enemy might attack by closely watching for signs of offensive action.

A wide variety of anti-personnel and anti-armour obstacles were employed. Maximum use was made of local and impounded materials. While it was difficult to conceal obstacles, the Germans would emplace barbed-wire barriers along natural contour lines, on low ground, on reverse slopes (*Hinterhang*), along the edge of fields and within vegetation. Terrain was important: swamps, marshes, forests, rivers, streams, gullies, ravines, broken and extremely rocky ground, all halted or slowed tanks. They fully understood that to be effective an obstacle had to be covered both by observation and fire.

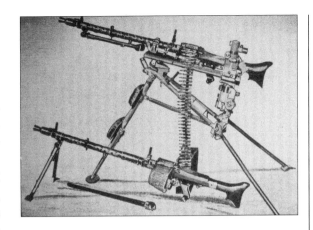

The 7.92mm MG.34 machine gun in the light and the heavy roles provided the weapon on which small unit defence tactics were centred. Maximum effective range of the MG.34 and the later MG.42 in the light role was 1,200m, although it was common to engage targets at much closer ranges. In the tripod-mounted heavy role, its range was 2,000m.

Obstacles

Hindernis	Obstacle
Astverhau	branch entanglement – tree or branch barrier
Baumstämmen	abatis – interlocked felled trees
Flanderzaun	'Flandrian fence' (**pictured**, *below left*) – double-apron barbed-wire, fence
Hindernisschlagpfahl	barbed-wire picket post
'K'/'S' Rolle	concertina wire – coiled spring, steel wire; 'K'= plain wire, 'S'= barbed wire
Koppelzäune	cattle fence – 4 or 5-strand barbed-wire fence
Panzerabwehrgraben	anti-armour ditch
Panzersperre aus Baumstämmen	armour barrier of [vertical] tree trunks
Pfahlsperre	stake barrier – featuring timber, log, or concrete posts
Schienensperre	rail barrier – vertically buried train rails
spanischer reiter	Spanish rider – portable wooden frame barrier wrapped in barbed wire (a.k.a. knife-rest, *chevaux de fries*)
Stacheldraht	barbed wire
Stahligeln	steel 'hedgehog' obstacle – three crossed girders
Straßensperre	roadblock – a general term
Stolperdranht-hindernis	trip-wire obstacle – low entangling wire

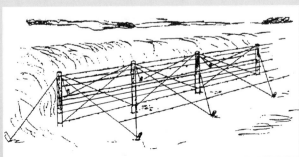

Planning the defences

Manuals provided standardised designs for field fortifications, but there were many variations and exceptions in the field. This was caused by the need to blend the fortification into the terrain, thus modifying its size, shape and profile; locally standardised designs induced by material shortages; types of material available; terrain conditions; weather; time constraints; preferences and concepts of local commanders; and the ingenuity and imagination of the officers and NCOs supervising construction. Many of the positions and structures specified in manuals were quite elaborate, though these tended to be the ideal standard. Dimensions, even of positions housing the same type of weapon, could vary. A common basic design can be seen in many examples though.

Establishing a defended area

A unit was assigned an area to defend based on terrain, vegetation, enemy forces, unit capabilities (most would be under strength and short of some crew-served weapons), and availability of reserves and supporting fire.

Depth and frontage

Infantry unit frontages could vary greatly (see Table 1). A major factor affecting the width of a division's sector was its internal organisation. Standard German infantry divisions had three infantry/grenadier regiments with three battalions each. (On 15 October 1942 all regiments and smaller units designated *Infanterie* were redesignated *Grenadier* for 'morale' purposes.) This allowed for the standard 'two up and one back' formation: that is, two subunits of any given unit were deployed in the main battle line with one behind them in reserve. From late-1943, due to manpower shortages, most infantry divisions were reorganised with only two battalions per regiment, and the reconnaissance battalion (*Aufklärungs-Abteilung*) was converted to a *Füsilier-Bataillon* as a mobile reserve. (The Germans employed two terms for 'battalion': *Bataillon* was used by infantry and pioneer battalions, and *Abteilung* or 'subdivision' was used by armour, artillery, smoke, cavalry and other branches.) This required regiments to place both battalions in the line without a reserve, although a company may have been retained as a regimental reserve. However, this meant that one of the battalions was without a reserve. Often all three regiments had to be in the line with only the fusilier battalion as the divisional reserve. In 1942

A Panzergrenadier-Division Grossdeutschland command post. The Germans relied heavily on telephones when defending. The equipment includes two Feldfernsprecher 33 field telephones and a Feldklappenschrank 20-line field switchboard.

Table 1: width of sector		
Unit	Metres	Yards
Squad	30–50	33–55
Platoon	200–450	220–550
Company	400–1,000	440–1,100
Battalion	800–2,000	880–2,200
Regiment	2,000–3,000	2,200–3,300
Division	6,000–10,000	6,600–11,000

combat-depleted divisions consolidated the remnants of their reconnaissance and anti-armour battalions into a single unit to serve as a mobile reserve (*Panzerjäger und Aufklärungs-Abteilung*). The separate battalions were later reconstituted. It was common for the only effective mobile reserve to be found at corps or army level. Mountain (*Gebirgs*) and light infantry (*Jäger*) divisions had only two regiments with three battalions, because they were expected to fight on rough terrain with narrow frontages. The 700-series occupation divisions raised in 1941 also had only two regiments and a single artillery battalion. Both of these divisional structures, three two-battalion regiments and two three-battalion regiments, greatly reduced a division's ability to defend in depth and field a viable reserve.

A *cheval de frise* used to close a roadblock. They were ineffective as anti-armour obstacles, but have been used as infantry and cavalry obstacles since ancient times.

The depth of each of the positions depended much on the terrain and likely avenues of enemy approach: there was no specified depth. Depth would be achieved by not only positioning the two subunits forward and the reserve subunit to the rear for each unit, but elements of each subunit might be deployed in depth within the position providing mutual support and protecting the flanks. Various crew-served weapons attached from higher formations added to the width and depth of positions as well.

The main battle line

The main battle line (*Hauptkampflinie*), analogous to the US 'main line of resistance', was determined by the commander using map reconnaissance. Subordinate unit commanders then reconnoitered the ground and moved their units into position. Commanders were cautioned not to spend too much time on reconnaissance so as not to delay construction of defences. They designated their subunit's area, primary sectors of fire, locations of support weapons, obstacles, minefields, command posts, aid stations, ammunition and supply points, and so on. The higher commander might specify the locations and sectors of fire of crew-served weapons allocated from higher formations in order to ensure their integration into the overall defence plan. Artillery, infantry gun and mortar fire-support plans were developed. Reserve positions were established and counter-attack plans made.

The 8cm mortar firing position was just large enough to accommodate three men and the mortar. An ammunition niche has been cut in the rear of the circular position. Armour protection trenches connect to both sides of the position. The 12cm mortar position was similar, but slightly larger.

The advanced position

The advanced position (*Vorgeschobene Stellung*) was established 4,500–6,500m forward of the main battle line. It would be manned by reconnaissance troops, detachments from reserve units, and anti-armour and machine gun subunits. Artillery forward observers would be located there, and the approaches forward of the position were within range of medium artillery (15cm): these could be employed to break up any attack. The forces were widely scattered and in shallow depth. Small troop elements covered the roads, trails and railways approaching the position, plus crossroads, river crossings, and key terrain such as high ground. They warned of enemy attack, prevented patrols from penetrating into

the main defences, attempted to force the enemy to deploy early, and called for fire on the enemy. The troops manning the advanced position would withdraw using concealed routes before they became too committed. The advanced position was not employed if the front was stabilised: that is, if enemy forces were in established positions or in close proximity to the German line.

Combat outposts

The combat outposts (*Gefechtsvorposten*) were 2,000–4,500m forward of the main battle line. While similar in concept to the US combat outpost line, they were often better manned. This sector had much the same mission as the advanced position, but might be more heavily armed and manned in stronger positions. It could mislead the enemy as to the location of the main battle line: dummy positions might be constructed for this purpose. Obstacles and minefields were placed on avenues of approach and covered by fire. The combat outposts were within light artillery (10.5cm) range and forward observers from the howitzer batteries were located in these positions Villages, tree lines and clumps, and hills covering the avenues of approach were developed as strongpoints. The Germans fully realised that enemy infantry would more than likely advance through woods and other terrain offering concealment rather than in the open, and so such areas were covered by reconnaissance patrols (*Spähtrupp*), outposts (*Vorposten*),

The standard German minefield warning sign was a black skull on a white background. Signs marked *Minen* were also used. These were normally only placed on the German side of minefields, although in areas where civilians were present they were placed all around the field with the aim of removing the signs prior to the Allies' arrival.

lookouts (*Feldwache*), observation posts (*Beobachtungstelle*), listening posts (*Horchstelle*) and fire. The same types of units manning the advanced position, especially if it was not employed, manned the combat outpost position: platoons and companies from the reserve regiment held the strongpoints here. They could also execute small-scale, limited-objective attacks to delay any enemy advance. The outposts were abandoned on order or when in danger of being overrun. Concealed withdrawal routes were selected so as not to interfere with covering artillery fire. Artillery and mortar fire was often registered on the forward positions to delay the enemy and cover the withdrawal. Artillery was usually emplaced approximately one-third of its maximum effective range behind the main battle line.

The main battlefield

The main battlefield (*Hauptkampffeld*) concentrated the bulk of the infantry and their supporting weapons on dominating terrain features or terrain that blocked or covered avenues of advance. Prior to 1942 the main battle position comprised mutually supporting platoon positions. Each company deployed two platoons forward and one in reserve. The reserve company of each battalion was similarly deployed to provide depth to the position. Light machine guns were deployed forward with riflemen, while heavy machine guns could be placed well forward, often slightly to the rear, covering gaps between units, possible enemy attack positions, and the flanks. Anti-armour rifles and light mortars (5cm) were located within the platoon positions to allow the gunners direct observation of targets. Heavy mortars (8cm) were placed on reverse slopes, as were infantry guns. Anti-armour guns were usually to the rear of forward positions and covering avenues of armour advance. Some anti-armour guns were emplaced in forward positions though. Mines were laid and obstacles constructed to the extent allowed by limits of time and *matériel*. These could be continuous belts laid in depth in well-developed positions.

A division with three three-battalion regiments would normally have two regiments in the main battle position with a total of four battalions forward.

This meant that eight of the division's 27 rifle companies were in the division's main battle line, each with two platoons forward. To all intents and purposes, the reserve platoons were in the battle line, as they were within sight of the forward platoons and supported them with direct fire. This meant that 24 of the division's 81 platoons were on the 6,000–10,000m frontline. The combat outpost position was manned by the forward regiments' reserve battalion and the advanced position, if established, was manned by detachments from the reserve regiment, reconnaissance and anti-tank troops.

The 3.7cm Pak.35/36 gun was the principal regimental anti-armour weapon, but was later supplemented by 5cm and 7.5cm weapons. The brick roadway leads to a dug-in position in which to conceal and protect the gun. Note that the roadway is lower where the gun fires from, a feature intended to lower its silhouette.

The strongpoint concept, December 1941

In December 1941 the Germans adopted a new defensive concept to deal with the desperate situation on the Eastern Front. The initial plan for the winter of 1941/42 was to drive the Red Army towards the Ural Mountains, seize the main population and industrial centres, and withdraw two-thirds of the German forces, leaving the rest to establish a line of strongpoints to defend the Third Reich's new frontier. The strongpoint defence was an economy-of-force effort to employ the smallest possible number of troops to cover the widest possible front. German losses had been tremendous and replacements could not be trained fast enough. Understrength units could not man the required wide fronts in the traditional manner – a near continuous linear defence. On 16 December Hitler issued his 'no retreat' order, putting a halt to local withdrawals then underway as units sought more easily defendable terrain in which to sit out the winter. The official term for a strongpoint was *Stützpunkt*, but Hitler preferred 'hedgehog position' (*Igelstellung*): *Stützpunkt* generally remained in use in official publications though.

The 'no retreat' order denied commanders a proven, effective countermeasure to massed Soviet attacks. Regardless of the order, it was still carried out in some instances. When a Soviet attack was imminent the forward troops were pulled back prior to the artillery barrages striking the strongpoints. Depending on the terrain, a withdrawal of 800–2,000m back to second-line positions was all that was required. The barrages fell on empty positions and obstacles, as Russian infantrymen rushed forward supported by tanks. The Germans would then open fire with artillery, mortars and machine guns from long range and wait for the assault's momentum to slow, formations to become disorganised and disorientated, and then to either withdraw or stumble piecemeal into the prepared defences. The forward positions could usually be reoccupied following German counter-attacks.

Army Group Centre had successfully employed the elastic defence in August and September, but by December German units were so severely under strength that such a defence could not be established other than as a thin screen. Sufficient troops were simply not available to man the multiple-zone, in-depth defence over such broad fronts, and the necessary mobile reserves did not exist. Panzer divisions fielded only a dozen tanks and the remaining crews were serving as infantrymen. Rear service units were stripped to provide infantry replacements. Infantry battalions were at less than company strength, and companies had 25–70 men. The infantry strength of entire corps was less than 2,000 troops with a 250-man battalion deemed well manned. Many units possessed only a quarter of their heavy weapons. Rather than the doctrinal

A rifle platoon in defensive position, early war

A rifle platoon in defensive position, early war

An early-war rifle platoon (*Zug*) defensive position is depicted here with all three squads (*Gruppe*, labelled A, B and C) deployed on line. 19 two-man rifle positions (1) are used. It was intended that the squad light machine guns (2) be positioned to cover the entire platoon front without gaps, but this was not always possible. Alternate machine-gun positions may have been prepared to cover gaps as well as the flanks and the gaps between adjacent platoons. Time permitting, some scattered rifle and one or two light machine-gun positions may have been dug in the rear and oriented in that direction (3). On this type of terrain the positions were typically at 10m intervals, less in densely wooded terrain. In some exceptional circumstances one squad may have been deployed to the rear, oriented forward, to provide depth to the position. If the platoon had four squads one would normally be deployed in the rear. The platoon's 5cm light mortar (4) is positioned to the rear, but in a place where it could observe its target area, as it had no observers. A 3.7cm anti-armour gun (5) and two heavy machine-gun squads (6) have been attached to the platoon along with an anti-armour rifle troop (7). The forward perimeter and flanks are protected by a double-apron barbed wire fence (a 'Flanders fence', 8) some 30–50m from the positions, keeping the troops beyond hand-grenade range. Sods of earth for camouflaging the positions have been removed in the rear from beneath trees and brush (9). The Zugführer's (10) and Zug-Truppführer's (11) positions are also indicated. An observation or listening post (12) is located to the front of the platoon, beyond the wire fence. The large red arrow (*feindwärts*) indicates the direction towards the enemy.

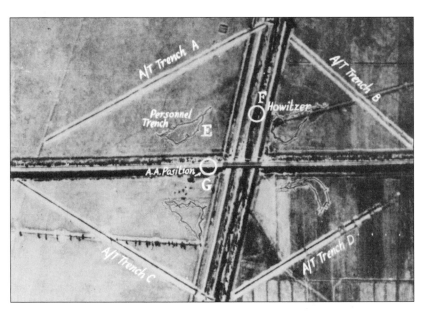

LEFT A road junction strongpoint in Germany made conspicuous by the straight anti-armour ditches (A–D). The hedge-lined roads are blocked by anti-armour mines. Fighting trenches (E) are located in each quadrant of the road intersection. A 7.5cm infantry gun (F) is positioned in a hedgerow and a 2cm flak gun (G), also positioned to engage ground targets, is beside the intersection.

BELOW A water-filled portion of the anti-armour ditch 'A' shown in the photograph on the left. The moat-like, water-filled ditch was an effective anti-personnel obstacle.

6–10km sectors, the hollow divisions were assigned 30–60km fronts against the unexpected Soviet counteroffensive. All three regiments had to be placed in the main battle line, with often all nine battalions as well, allowing no regimental reserves other than the battalions' reserve companies, which were also manning deeper strongpoints. The Germans called it 'putting everything in the shop window'. Scattered squads and platoons would be held in reserve by battalions and companies to conduct immediate, local counter-attacks. An under-strength reconnaissance battalion served as the division's only mobile reserve, although if possible divisions retained one infantry battalion in reserve. To make matters worse, the strained German logistics system was on the verge of collapse.

Under-strength companies might organise into two platoons with three 6–10-man squads, each

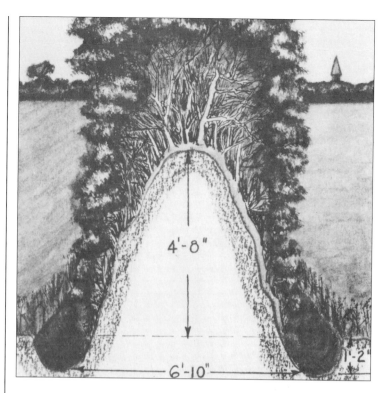

A cross-section of a typical Normandy hedgerow (the precise dimensions would vary). The core of the hedgerows comprised rocks gathered by previous generations and piled in lines along the edges of fields. Thick hedges then grew over these berms. The dense roots and rock core made the hedgerows formidable anti-armour and anti-personnel obstacles. They also provided ideal fighting positions.

with a machine gun and positioned in a cluster of 3–5 two-man firing positions. Additional machine guns were often provided from service units as a substitute for riflemen. Remaining 5cm mortars were concentrated 50m to the rear under company control. Anti-armour guns were held in the rear to deal with tank breakthroughs. In some instances anti-armour guns were placed in strongpoints, making few available to block breakthroughs in the rear.

Strongpoints were established around villages to control roads and provide shelter from the brutal weather until fighting positions and bunkers could be built. Other strongpoints were built on the little available high ground. Weapons were positioned to engage the enemy at maximum range, provide mutual support to adjacent strongpoints, and cover the gaps between strongpoints.

The little remaining artillery was positioned further forward than normal, increasing the danger of it being overrun, to cover the different strongpoints. Many divisions fielded only an under-strength artillery battalion, rather than four, causing the few batteries to be widely dispersed to cover all the strongpoints. This prevented artillery fire from being concentrated en masse on main attacks, as not all batteries could range the wide division front. Mortars were distributed among strongpoints rather than being concentrated behind the forward units, meaning they were unable to range all the strongpoints. They could usually cover adjacent strongpoints though. Light air-defence units positioned their 2cm flak guns in strongpoints, which proved ideal for breaking up mass infantry attacks.

The strongpoint defence remained into mid-1943/1944 in some areas. After that the Germans were in steady retreat. Defences consisted of hastily established lines in scattered sectors without continuous frontlines, little depth, and few if any reserves. As relentless Allied assaults hammered at the Germans on all fronts, time and resources rarely allowed anything close to a doctrinal defence to be established. Pioneer units often built defensive positions and obstacles to await withdrawing infantry. Defences were built on rivers to provide major obstacles; villages and towns were turned into strongpoints and cities into 'fortresses' (*Festung*, essentially a propaganda title). Some of these, though, were well defended with multiple rings of strongpoints protected by anti-armour ditches and minefields. In-depth defences were prepared on the roads leading into the fortress city. Switch positions were constructed between the fortified lines to protect against breakthroughs.

Hedgerow defences, Normandy 1944

In Normandy the Germans encountered a compartmented maze of cultivated fields, orchards and pastures atop the Collines de Normandie plateau 10–15 kilometres inland (the Bocage country). These fields were separated by earth and rock berms 0.5–1.5m thick and up to 1.5m high. They were topped with dense hedges and small trees from 1m to 5m in height. Ditch-lined roads and wagon tracks, often sunken, ran throughout the area bounded on both sides by

This aerial view of the Normandy Bocage shows how the hedgerows were devoid of formal patterns. Utah Beach is just off the bottom of the photo. The dark areas are cloud shadows.

hedgerows with small, gated openings into the fields. The enclosed fields could be relatively small up to a few hundred metres to a side. They could be square, rectangular or triangular and were laid out in irregular patterns.

The Germans dug weapon positions and riflemen holes, often with an attached dugout, into the hedgerows as well as dugouts and positions for command posts, telephone exchanges, ammunition points, medical stations and others. Well camouflaged, they were difficult to detect from the ground or air. Observation between fields was impossible and an attacking force had no idea what was behind the next or adjacent hedgerows. The only way to approach a hedgerow was by crossing the open fields. The Germans would dig positions along the far side of the hedgerow and those on the flanks in

A slit trench adjacent to a 10.5cm howitzer position in a Normandy hedgerow. While the howitzer's position was well concealed, the slit trench was poorly camouflaged, a fact that helped aerial photo interpreters detect the battery's position.

the defended sectors. There were no continuous straight lines, consisting more of a chequerboard pattern. Allied tactics evolved with alternating fields attacked with tank support while mortars and artillery suppressed the intervening fields' hedgerows. Hedgerow-cutter ploughs were fabricated for attachment to tanks, allowing them to burst through the berms. The compartmented nature of the hedgerows allowed the Germans to break contact easily though, and withdraw to the next hedgerow.

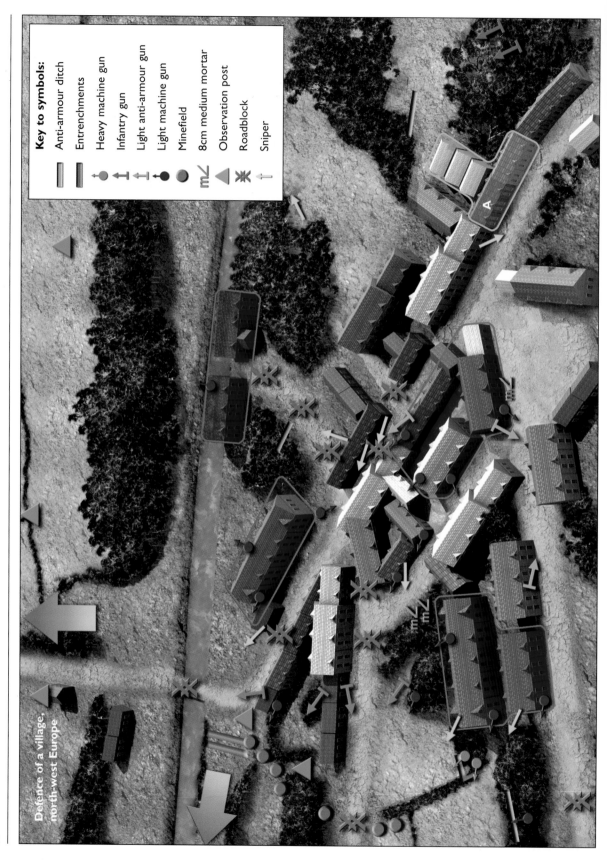

Key to symbols:

Anti-armour ditch
Entrenchments
Heavy machine gun
Infantry gun
Light anti-armour gun
Light machine gun
Minefield
8cm medium mortar
Observation post
Roadblock
Sniper

Defence of a village, north-west Europe

LEFT Defence of a village, north-west Europe

Villages were extremely irregular in pattern and layout, making the organisation of the defence, the selection of strongpoints, the positioning of crew-served weapons, and the placement of obstacles as difficult for the defender to determine as for the attacker to predict. There were endless possibilities. Light defences and observation posts were positioned on the village's outskirts. In this example, significant anti-armour defences are positioned on the outer edge to the left to blunt an expected tank penetration. These anti-armour guns would have alternate positions deeper in the village. Most strongpoints are located well within the village and machine gunners and snipers (in reality selected riflemen) are scattered through the village to disrupt and delay the attackers. Mortars and infantry guns are positioned to fire on all main approaches and they too have alternate positions in the event of the attacker approaching them. The strongpoints consist of interconnected defended groups of barricaded buildings with concealed firing positions, reinforced cellars and mouse holes connecting buildings. Two of the main roads through the village are left unblocked to allow attacking tanks to enter killing zones within the village. Anti-armour guns repositioned from the outer defence line to the left will cover these. The reserve platoon is located at **A**. Strongpoints are shown enclosed within red lines.

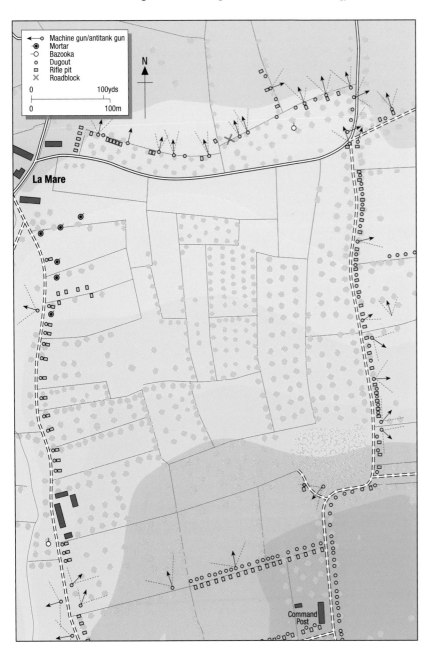

Hedgerow defences, Normandy, 1944. The faint lines represent the hedgerows and the double broken lines are sunken roads. This c. 300m × 800m company area was self-contained and could fend off attacks from any direction. Note that the buildings were undefended, as they attracted artillery fire. If the perimeter were penetrated, troops would move to the flanking hedgerows to engage the attackers. There were several clusters of positions located in adjacent hedgerows on all sides of this area.

Defensive firepower

The infantry regiment

The German infantry regiment was a well-structured unit with a complete range of support weapons allocated to all subunits. The types of automatic weapons, mortars and infantry guns were well balanced. The main flaw was inadequate anti-armour weapons, but attempts were made to improve them through the war. With one minor exception, the subunits at all levels were organised in triangular form and most support weapons were allocated so as to provide one weapon or a pair of weapons to each subordinate unit.

While the German Army was oriented towards mobile, offensive warfare, the infantry regiments, comprising the bulk of the combat power, still went largely by foot, with only small numbers of trucks and numerous horse-drawn wagons and carts to haul supplies and equipment.

There were numerous types of infantry regiments including mountain, light infantry, motorised infantry, and occupation or static troops. They were based on the same structure as the following standard 1939 infantry regiment, the basic common organisation. There were exceptions, depending on when the regiment was raised, including minor changes in weapons allocation, substitution of certain weapons by others, and slight differences of subunit organisation. The later two-battalion regiments mirrored this basic structure. Strengths are approximate, since units were habitually undermanned, thus rendering the authorised strength virtually meaningless.

The 3,250-man infantry regiment consisted of a staff section with mounted (on horseback, but soon replaced by bicycles), pioneer and signal platoons (*Zug*); a light infantry column (*leichte Infanterie Kolonne* – supplies, ammunition, baggage transport); I–III infantry battalions (*Bataillon*); and infantry gun and armour defence companies (*Kompanie*).

The 850-man battalions possessed a staff section with signal platoon and trains (*Troß*), three rifle companies and a machine-gun company. The companies were numbered in sequence through the regiment: I, 1st–4th companies; II, 5th–8th; and III, 9th–12th. The 4th, 8th, and 12th companies were machine-gun armed. The machine-gun company (*Machinegewehr-Kompanie*) had a company troop (*Kompanie-Trupp* – company headquarters), three heavy machine-gun platoons and a heavy-mortar platoon. The machine-gun platoons had three squads, each of two troops, with each manning a 7.92mm MG.38 tripod-mounted machine gun for a total of 12 guns. The mortar platoon had three squads, each with two troops, for a total of six 8cm s.Gr.W.34. (English-language publications refer to machine-gun and mortar squads – *Gruppe* – and troops – *Trupp* – as sections and squads, respectively, as they would be termed in a US organisation.)

The 190-man rifle (*Schützen*) companies had a company troop and trains (combat, rations, baggage), three rifle platoons, plus an anti-armour rifle squad. The 48-man rifle platoons had a platoon leader, an NCO troop leader (equivalent to a platoon sergeant), two messengers and a medical orderly in the platoon troop (*Zug-Trupp*). The platoon had a three-man light mortar troop with a 5cm le.Gr.W.36 mortar intended to engage machine-gun nests and small groups of infantrymen. There were initially four 10-man squads

Divisional artillery ranges

A division artillery regiment had three battalions (*Artillerie-Abteilung*) each with twelve 10.5cm howitzers (pictured below), the standard divisional light artillery piece. (There was no 8.8cm artillery piece, despite this being often stated: 8.8cm flak guns were used for anti-armour fire, but not in the indirect fire role.) The 7.5cm gun, which had been replaced by the 10.5cm prior to the war, was reissued late in the war and was a poor substitute for the 10.5cm. The regiment also had a battalion with twelve 15cm howitzers and four 10cm (actually 105mm) guns for long-range counter-battery fire.

Artillery	Range
7.5cm le.F.K.18, light field gun	9,425m
10.5cm le.F.H.18, light field howitzer	10,675m
15cm s.F.H.18, heavy field howitzer	13,325m
10cm s.K.18, heavy gun	19,015m

with a squad leader, troop leader (assistant squad leader), machine gunner, his assistant, an ammunition man, and five riflemen. The three-man MG.34 light machine-gun troop operated under the squad leader's control. The riflemen operated as the rifle troop under the direct control of the troop leader. The squad leader had a 9mm MP.38 or MP.40 machine pistol, the machine gunner a 9mm P.08 Luger or P.38 Walther pistol, while all the others had 7.92mm Kar.98k Mauser carbines. One rifleman had a rifle grenade launcher, and two hand grenades were carried by most men.

Machine guns

A brief discussion of light and heavy machine guns is in order. The MG.34 and later MG.42 machine guns served in many roles. In German practice, the terms 'light' and 'heavy' defined the machine gun's role, not its weight. In the light machine-gun role the weapon was used on its bipod or fired from the hip or shoulder. It provided half the rifle squad's firepower and the squad's manoeuvre tactics and defence were centred on the gun. The three-man troop carried one spare barrel. In the heavy machine-gun role the weapon was manned by a six-man troop, mounted on a tripod, provided with a long-range optical sight, and had three spare barrels to provide supporting long-range overhead and flanking fire.

An MG.34 machine gun in the embrasure of an Eastern Front bunker. The firing port is made from boards and snow-filled wicker ammunition containers.

The company's seven-man anti-armour rifle squad had three 7.92mm Pz.B.39 *Panzerbüchse* anti-armour rifles. By 1941 this weapon was obsolete, but remained in limited use for a time. It used a 7.92 x 94mm cartridge, much larger than the 7.92 x 57mm used in carbines and machine guns (the second number indicates the case length). Other models were used, including captured weapons.

Infantry artillery

The 13th Infantry Gun (*Infanteriegeschütz*) Company possessed a headquarters, signal section, two light-gun platoons and a heavy-gun platoon. Its armament comprised four 7.5cm le.IG.18 light infantry guns and two 15cm s.I.G33 heavy infantry guns, two per platoon. These were short-range howitzers manned by infantrymen, and could provide immediate indirect and low-angle fire for the regiment without having to rely on divisional artillery, thus ensuring any attack's momentum was maintained. The 14th Armour Defence (*Panzerabwehr*) Company, Anti-armour (*Panzerjäger*) from April 1940, had four platoons, each with four 3.7cm Pak.35/36 anti-armour guns and a light machine gun troop. These companies remained designated 13th and 14th even in two-battalion regiments. The tactical allocation of these weapons in the defence has already been discussed in the *Planning the defences* chapter.

Machine-gun bunkers were built in many forms. This version provided a relatively small position for a light machine gun. It had minimal space for the two-man crew, protected from light-mortar and small-arms fire, and was difficult to detect if properly camouflaged.

As new divisions were raised during the first three years of the war, there were many variations in regimental subunit organisation and weapon allocation. Rifle platoons were fielded with three rather than four squads, but

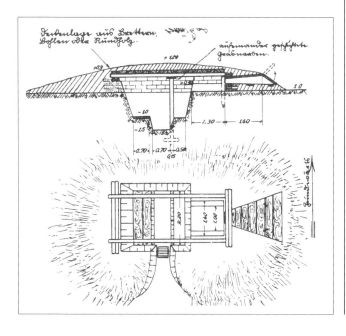

Three Fallschirmjägern fire an 8cm Gr.W.34 mortar from a standard mortar firing position.

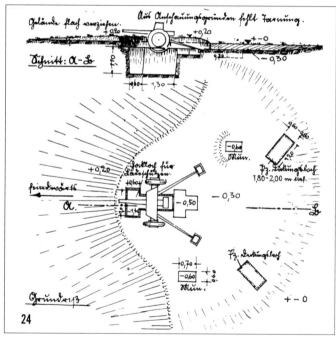

Anti-armour gun positions could be circular, oval or hastily prepared as here. Ammunition niches have been dug to the rear, as have armour protection trenches. A slit trench has also been dug beneath the gun.

the company received a heavy machine-gun squad with two MG.34s. This soon disappeared and all platoons had three squads. Many units were raised without the 5cm mortar in each rifle platoon or the three company anti-armour rifles. Other battalions lacked the machine-gun company's 8cm mortar platoon. Some regiments were fielded with a 15th Pioneer Company, but they were soon withdrawn and organised into pioneer battalions.

From 1940 regiments were being raised with the infantry gun company having only four 7.5cm guns. Other regiments had no regimental companies or battalion machine-gun companies, merely a heavy company (*schweren-Kompanie*) in each battalion with four light infantry guns and four 3.7cm anti-armour guns. In 1942 on the Eastern Front the 13th Infantry Gun Company began to be replaced by a mortar company with eight captured Soviet 12cm HM38 mortars: the Germans soon began manufacturing a direct copy, the 12cm Gr.W.42. The 13th Mortar (*Grantwerfer*) Company became a fixture in most regiments. The 3.7cm *Torklopfer* ('door-knocker') anti-armour guns began to be replaced by 5cm Pak.38 guns in 1940/41. While the 7.5cm Pak.40 was intended for divisional and corps/army-level anti-armour battalions, some found their way to infantry regiments. The 5cm mortars were withdrawn from use in late-1943 for being impotent. They were replaced by short-barrelled 8cm Gr.W.42, which may or may not have been received. In late-1942, the one-shot, disposable, anti-armour *Panzerfaust* ('Armour-fist') rocket launcher began to appear and by the end of the following year was in wide use. They were issued to riflemen as needed and did not require crew.

Late-war restructuring

The new-type 1944 infantry division saw the loss of a battalion from each regiment – a 45 per cent strength reduction, to 1,987 men per regiment. The

7.5cm and 15cm infantry gun positions comprised a circular pit with armour protection trenches on two sides. This one has a low berm behind the exit ramp and ammunition niches are located to either side and to the rear.

A partially completed position for a 7.5cm Pak.40 anti-armour gun. Constructed in an open field, its low profile would reduce the gun's outline, although this did limit the field of fire.

184-man regimental staff included signal, pioneer (six le.MG.) and cyclist (three le.MG.) platoons plus small trains. The 708-man battalions each had three 142-man rifle companies, a 205-man machine-gun company, and 65 men in the staff section and trains. The rifle companies had 16 light machine guns and two 8cm mortars. The machine-gun companies had three platoons each with four heavy machine guns or two four-gun platoons and a platoon with two 2cm Flak.38 automatic guns, plus a platoon with four 12cm mortars. The 13th Infantry Gun Company had six 7.5cm and two 15cm infantry guns, although these were in short supply. The 14th Anti-armour Company had three platoons of four heavy anti-armour guns, which could have been the 7.5cm Pak.40, 7.5cm Pak.97/38 (French 75mm barrels on Pak.38 carriages) or 7.62cm Pak.36(r) (captured Soviet M1936 field guns modified for the anti-armour role), the latter being in extremely wide use. In reality they usually had fewer guns and some may have been substituted by 5cm guns.

The People's Grenadier (*Volks-Grenadier*) divisions fielded in late-1944 also had only two battalions per regiment. The grenadier companies had only two 'machine-pistol' platoons, each with four light machine guns and no other crew-served weapons. In theory the platoons were supposed to be armed with

An artillery position might be dug in this triangular style, but circular, oval, and square pits were used as well. A dug-in artillery position was comparatively large to allow the 8–10-man crew to function. Ammunition niches are dug into the position's front and others would be located to the rear. A ramp to the rear allows the gun to be removed.

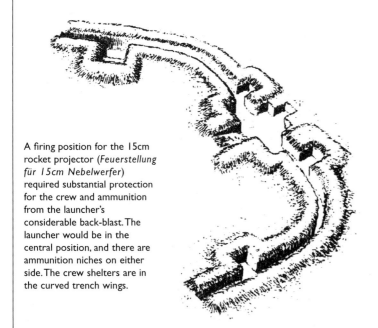

A firing position for the 15cm rocket projector (*Feuerstellung für 15cm Nebelwerfer*) required substantial protection for the crew and ammunition from the launcher's considerable back-blast. The launcher would be in the central position, and there are ammunition niches on either side. The crew shelters are in the curved trench wings.

7.92mm MP.43/Stg.44 assault rifles. (Originally the MP.43 was designated a machine pistol, but in 1944 it was redesignated an assault rifle to better describe its role and prevent confusion when requesting ammunition – other machine pistols were 9mm. The MP.43/Stg.44 used a 7.92 × 33mm round, shorter than that used in carbines and machine guns.) Platoons of this period often still had Kar.98k carbines, sometimes with a single semi-automatic 7.92mm G.43 rifle per squad. The battalion heavy companies (4th and 8th) had two four-gun heavy machine-gun platoons and a platoon of six 8cm mortars. The 13th Infantry Gun Company had four light infantry guns in two platoons, two of which may have been substituted by heavy guns, plus two mortar platoons with four 12cm mortars each. The 14th Armour Destroyer (*Panzerzerstörer*) Company had up to 54 shoulder-fired 8.8cm R.PzB.43 or 54 *Panzerschreck* ('Armour-terror') rocket launchers, an enlarged version of the US bazooka. It had three platoons with 18 launchers in three squads. Some companies had a platoon with three 7.5cm anti-armour guns.

The 1945 infantry division's regiments were similarly organised, but the battalion heavy companies (4th, 8th, 12th) had only two light infantry guns and eight 8cm mortars (no machine guns) while the regimental 13th Heavy Company had a platoon with two heavy infantry guns and eight 12cm mortars in two platoons. The 14th Company now had 18 spare *Panzerschreck* rocket-launchers

There were numerous corps- and army-level units that could be deployed in immediate support behind or with the frontline infantry to thicken the line. These included machine-gun (48 heavy), heavy mortar (36 × 12cm), anti-armour (36 × 7.5cm), light air defence (36 single and 9 quad 2cm, 12 × 3.7cm), heavy air defence (24 × 8.8cm), assault-gun (18 guns) and pioneer battalions. Late in the war, machine-gun battalions were often employed in the frontline in lieu of infantry units. This provided significant automatic-weapon fire and allowed in-depth positioning, but these units had limited counter-attack ability and possessed few anti-armour guns and mortars.

Materials and construction methods

The Germans made extensive use of local materials to build fortifications and obstacles. Concrete (*Beton*) was always prized for any fortification. Its value was realised after the Allies began bombing the Atlantikwall defences in 1943: field positions and trenches were destroyed while reinforced concrete (*Stahlbeton*) positions were virtually unscathed. However, concrete and reinforcing bar were rarely available in the field, as these were being diverted to the construction of the Atlantikwall, Westwall, Ostwall, U-boat pens, flak towers, bomb shelters, command bunkers and underground factories. Other available construction materials were insufficient, and were diverted to priority installations. The available local materials were dependent on the area of operations, with some offering abundant supplies (as in north-west Europe, Italy and parts of the USSR) and others (such as North Africa and the steppes of Russia) barren.

Timber

Timber (*Holz*) was abundant in Europe and parts of Russia. Many of the plans for field fortifications, shelters and obstacles provided in German manuals called for the extensive use of logs. 20–25cm-diameter logs (*Rundholz*) or 16 × 16cm cured timbers (*Bauholz*) were recommended for overhead cover, horizontal support beams (stringers), and vertical support posts. Dimensioned wooden planks (*Holzbrettern*) was used sparingly for revetting, flooring, doors, shutters, duckboards, ammunition niches, ladders and steps. Pioneer and construction units operated portable sawmills to cut lumber. Bunks, tables, benches and other furniture were also made from this and discarded ammunition boxes. Nails, especially the large type required for timber construction, were often scarce.

Revettments

The exterior of timber fortifications was banked with earth or buried below ground level. However, large-calibre penetrating projectiles could create deadly wood splinters. To reduce the risk of this, branches and saplings were woven horizontally like wicker (*Fletchwerk*) through 10cm vertical stakes or bundled brushwood fascines (*Faschinen*) to create supporting revettments (*Verkleidung*). The vertical stakes could be reinforced by securing anchor wires (*Drahtanker*) near the top and fastening them to shorter driven stakes a metre or so from the trench's edge.

Like all other armies, the Germans shipped munitions, rations and other *matériel* in robust wooden boxes and crates of all sizes. Wicker basket containers were also used, especially for artillery ammunition and propellant charges. These were often filled with earth and stacked like bricks to form interior walls of fortifications and for parapet revetting. They were braced by logs or timber or bound together by wire (*Draht*) to prevent their collapse when the fortification was struck by artillery. Boxes were also disassembled and the boards used to construct firing ports, doors, shelves, and the like. Nails removed from these boxes became a valuable

An M4 Sherman tank passes through a vertical log armour barrier inside a German village. The logs were buried as deep as 2m, and angled logs were sometimes set on the enemy's side to deflect any tank aiming to ram the German barriers. They required large quantities of demolition charges to breach them, as has been accomplished here.

Building a log machine-gun bunker

Building a log machine-gun bunker

The log machine-gun bunker (*Machinegewehr-Schartenstand aus Rundholz*) was loosely based on larger concrete fortifications on the Westwall. The bunker's firing port (FP) was oriented perpendicular to the enemy's expected line of advance in order to engage him from the flank. This allowed positions to have a thicker than normal wall on the enemy side, and to inflict a surprise attack from an unexpected direction: it also made it much easier to conceal the bunker. The interior included a battle room (*Kampf-Raum*, 1) for the light machine gun (a tripod-mounted heavy machine gun could be installed); an adjacent ammunition room (*Munitions-Raum*, 2); and an entry alcove (*Vorraum*, 3). A communications trench (4) connected it to other positions. The double-log walls were filled with rock or packed earth (5). The roof was made of multiple layers of logs, clay, rocks and earth (6). The sides and roof were covered over with sods of turf and care was taken to ensure it blended into the terrain.

The large red arrow on the main illustration indicates the direction towards the enemy (*feindwärts*): bunkers of this type were also built with the firing port oriented forward. Image A below shows the bunker in plan view; image B shows the bunker with its full earthern covering in place, without cutaway details; and image C depicts an alternative method used to mate the corners of log walls.

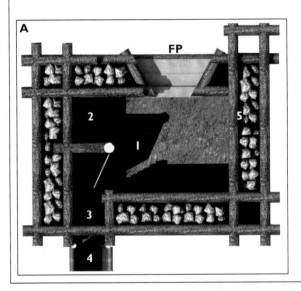

commodity. German munitions (including grenades, mines and mortar rounds) were often transported in comparatively expensive metal containers (*Muntionsbehälter*). While they were supposed to be returned to the factories for reuse, they were sometimes filled with earth and used for shoring up parapets. Steel fuel and oil drums were available, although they too were supposed to be returned. British three-gallon petrol tins were much used in North Africa, being filled with earth and used to revet parapets.

Purpose-made cloth sandbags (*Sandsäcke*) were scarce at the front as most production remained in Germany and in other rear areas. They were usually burlap tan, brown or grey. Other cloth shipping bags were used instead. Two layers of sandbags were sufficient to stop small-arms fire and provide protection from mortars.

Fortifications with firing ports, which needed to be above ground level, were kept as low as possible. Banked earth was piled high on the sides and angled at a fairly steep slope to absorb armour-piercing projectiles and the blast and fragmentation of high explosives. Layers of logs were sometimes laid just below the surface of the side banking as a burster layer. The above-ground portion of covered fortifications tended to be uniform rather than irregular.

Rocks and other materials

Rocks (*Stein*) were used for fortifications wherever they could be found, but were especially common in North Africa and Italy, where fortifications were often constructed entirely of this. Rocks and logs were laid in layers beneath the piled-earth overhead covering to act as shell burster material. Rocks were also used as in-fill between double log walls to detonate projectiles or deform armour-piercing rounds. One particular hazard to the occupants was from fragments caused by bullet and shell strikes. Trenches and positions were sometimes revetted with rock walls, but unless stakes and horizontal bracing or wire mesh were used to anchor this, a near miss artillery round could make it collapse.

Materials such as corrugated sheet metal, lumber, timbers, roofing tiles and shingles, doors, masonry, structural steel, pipes, railroad rails, concrete and steel railroad ties were frequently salvaged from local structures.

On the Eastern Front, ice (*Eis*) and frozen snow (*Schnee*) proved to be ideal for fortifications and shelters. The duration and average depth of snowfall varied depending on the region. In the north it began in December, accumulated 100cm or more, and remained into June. In the south it began in January and remained until April with only 10–40cm falling. Temperatures remained 20–50°F below zero through the winter. Ice blocks and packed snow were surprisingly bulletproof, and simple to work. They required no revetting, but bails of hay or straw were sometimes used to support trenches and walls and to provide additional insulation. The protective thickness of frozen materials from small-arms bullet penetration is shown in Table 2.

A 15cm heavy infantry gun in a log-revetted firing position. To the left of the weapon a gunner digs an armour protection trench within the position.

The principles of construction

Detailed and elaborate plans for the construction of field fortifications, shelters and obstacles were provided, and many of the principles on which they were based had been developed in World War I. Even though time and resources did not always allow these ideal positions to be built, they served as guides and their influence can be seen in the design of those actually constructed. A great deal of local initiative was used.

For the most part defensive positions were dug as deep as possible and kept low to the ground in order to present a low profile, both for concealment and to offer less of a target. Positions not requiring firing ports were usually flush with the ground. This was not always possible because of a high water table, swampy ground or shallow bedrock. In such instances the position had to be completely above ground level. In addition, the roof had to protect the position from heavy artillery: its thickness might also mean that the position's profile was not always as low as desired. In some instances the firing port had to be well above the ground in order to cover its field of fire effectively, especially if firing downhill, which could also raise the position's profile. Positions dug into the sides of hills, ridges, gorges and the like were usually built flush with the surface if possible, making them difficult to detect when camouflaged.

Most covered positions and shelters were built from logs, usually laid horizontally and with the ends notched for assembly, or spiked together.

Table 2: protective thickness of frozen materials	
Frozen material	**Thickness**
Loose snow	120cm
Packed snow	80cm
Snow with ice crust	40–60cm
Ice	28cm
Frozen ground	20cm
Frozen clay	15cm

Horizontally constructed log walls were supported by vertical pilings with the ends often held together by steel staples. Wire was sometimes used to bind logs together. The upper ends of vertical load-bearing support posts were sometimes bound by wire to prevent the end from splintering from high explosive impacts. Interior walls were built of logs, planks, woven branches and saplings, rock, sandbags or hay bales to prevent collapse when hit by artillery or bombs.

Overhead cover (*In deckung*) comprised a layer of large-diameter logs with a second layer laid perpendicular to them on top. Manuals called for no more than two or three layers, but in practice up to half a dozen layers could be used to ensure protection from heavy artillery. Waterproof roofing felt (tarpaper, *Dachpappe*), if available, was laid atop the roofing logs before they were covered with earth. A 5cm layer of clay was sometimes laid over the logs providing marginal waterproofing. If above ground, sods or peat blocks were stacked brick-like to shore up the angled sides. The whole fortification was covered over with sods removed from the site before digging began. If needed, additional sods were brought for the rear. This was supposed to be removed from areas beneath trees and brush so that it was undetectable from the air. While the manuals provided precise dimensions for fortifications, they often did not specify the thickness of overhead cover. This depended on how deep the position could be dug: the deeper it was, the thicker the overhead cover. Examples of specified overhead thickness are 160cm for a below-ground squad bunker and 130cm for an above-ground machine-gun bunker. The spacing of vertical support posts and stringer logs varied from approximately 1m to 1.5m.

A quad AA machine-gun position protecting an airfield from low-level attack. The sides are revetted with tree branches and the gun mounted on a concrete pedestal. The position is about 2.5m in diameter and 1.5m deep. This expedient weapon was assembled in large numbers during 1944–45 from surplus 7.92mm MG.17 aircraft machine guns.

Light mortars (US 60mm, UK 2in., USSR 50mm) did not possess the ability to penetrate most bunkers. Medium mortars (US 81mm, UK 3in., USSR 82mm) were more effective, but heavy mortars (US/UK 4.2in., USSR 120mm) were best suited, especially since they sometimes had delay fuses. Light artillery (75mm, 105mm, 25pdr) had limited effect, whereas medium artillery, like the 155mm, could destroy a well-prepared bunker.

Firing ports or embrasures (*Schießscharte*) were kept small to make them more difficult to detect and hit. A 60° field of fire (*Wirkungsbereich*) was recommended, but the angle could be narrower or wider. The ports were made of smaller-diameter logs, planks or sandbags. There was usually only one firing port; seldom did additional ports exist to cover alternate sectors. These were usually placed very low to the ground, if not flush with it.

Open-topped (*offen*) fighting positions such as rifleman's holes, trenches and holes for machine guns, mortars, infantry guns and anti-tank guns, were kept as small as possible. Small positions, just large enough to accommodate the weapon and crew and allow them to function effectively, required less construction time and camouflage, were more difficult to detect, especially from the air, and made a smaller target. Manuals called for trenches to be 60–80cm wide at the top and 40cm wide at the bottom, providing slightly sloped sides. In practice they tended to be narrower if the soil was stable enough to support it, with the sides almost vertical. They were either without an earth parapet (*Brustwehr*) or had a very low parapet for concealment. Parapets were used if the hardness of the soil, a lack of time, or a high water table did not allow the positions to be dug sufficiently deep. It also required

This 3.7cm Flak36 gun emplacement was located outside a forced-labour camp at Waldorf, Germany. It remains mounted on its wheeled carriage, although its precious tires have been removed, probably for use on trucks. Revetted with saplings and banked with earth, no effort was made to camouflage the position.

significant time and effort to remove the spoil, conceal it, and return the ground around the position to a natural state.

The idea of removing soil and keeping the position level with the ground was learned from the Italians in North Africa. On flat, barren desert floors natural features and vegetation were non-existent and concealment was achieved by blending the positions into the ground. For machine-gun positions the Italians developed an underground shell-proof shelter and magazine with a small circular chamber. Its ceiling tapered to a neck, serving as the machine-gun position. The 'Tobruk pit' (*Tobukstellung* or *Ringständ*) provided a small, circular, difficult to detect opening with 360° fire for the machine gun. Separate entrances were provided or they were connected to central bunkers by tunnels. The Germans developed similar positions for the 5cm mortar and one mounting a tank turret, the *Panzerstellung*. While they were often built of timber, concrete ones were sometimes encountered in critical front sectors, as they required little cement. These and similar small concrete positions were categorised as reinforced field works. Concrete Tobruk pits were common on the Atlantikwall.

Entrances to positions were normally in the rear, but in some instances they might be on the side of a position depending on the protection and concealment afforded by surrounding terrain. Entrances were often protected to prevent direct fire, blast fragmentation, grenades and demolitions from entering. This might be in the form, of a blast barrier inside the position, or a similar barrier or wall on the outside. A trench with at least one right-angle turn usually formed the entry passage. Many positions though had only a straight, unprotected entry way. This often proved to be the srongest defensive point: if the attackers gained the position's rear, they would usually come under fire from adjacent positions. Larger positions often had a vestibule or entry hallway (*Vorraum*) separated from the main compartment by a log wall.

A square 3.7cm Flak36 gun emplacement made of concrete, with much of the formation planking left in place. Some effort was made to camouflage-paint the emplacement's sides. Ammunition and gun equipment niches were built into the interior sides. The gun's wheeled carriage was removed and the jack-stands set on earth-filled ammunition boxes. A second emplacement can just be seen in the background, to the left of the US soldier. Such weapons were usually employed in threes.

LEFT This 15cm s.IG.33 heavy infantry-gun position blends well with the surrounding rocky Italian terrain. The haphazardly constructed rectangular rock parapet looks like just another pile of rocks. The gun was painted dark yellow, common after 1943, and sprayed with green paint. The camouflage pattern actually calls attention to the weapon though, as it outlines rather than disrupts the shape of the shield.

BELOW This rock and log personnel shelter was to the rear of the 15cm infantry-gun position shown in the picture above. Its narrow entrance and the fact that it has been built around a couple of trees made it difficult to detect.

This helped protect occupants from grenades and demolition charges as well as from external blast overpressure and chemical agents. This also served as a changing area for wet clothes and helped keep out cold draughts as troops entered and exited for guard duty and patrols.

Frontline open positions for crew-served weapons were provided with armour protective trenches (*Panzerdeckungslöchern*), or simply 'armour trenches' (*Panzergraben*). These were narrow, deep slit trenches on either side of the position – 'wings' that provided cover for the crew if overrun by tanks. Often they would be dug with an angled turn, in the form of a wide 'V'. For protection from the crushing action of a tank, the trench had to provide 75cm of clearance above the crouching occupants. They were also used if the position came under artillery or mortar fire, or air attack, as well as for firing positions for close-in defence. Ideally these would be covered if time and resources permitted.

Ammunition niches (*Munitionslöchern*) were dug into the sides of trenches and other positions, and usually a wooden box was inserted there. Anti-armour gun, infantry gun, and artillery positions had ammunition niches dug into the ground at an angle and lined with a box with a lid. These were located a minimum of 10m to the rear of the position.

Eingraben!

Infantrymen were issued a small entrenching tool (*kleines Schanzzeug*), with a fixed square blade and short wood handle. The folding spade (*Klappspaten*) had a longer wood handle and a pointed blade, and it saw less use: the 1943 US folding entrenching tool was based on this model. Both types were carried in leather carriers attached to the belt over the left hip. The signal for showing 'We are dug in' was to hold one's entrenching tool above one's head with the back of the blade facing forward. The signal for showing 'We are digging in' was to hold the front of the blade forward. Troop units were issued long-handled rounded spades, pickaxes, axes, hatchets and hoes for building field fortifications. Since there were often shortages, confiscated civilian tools and captured items were also employed. Wire-cutters, handsaws, hammers and mallets were also provided. Pioneer troops were issued similar spades and pickaxes with detachable handles. The blade or pickaxe head was carried in a leather carrier: both this and the handle were attached to backpacks. Pioneer troops occasionally used two-man petrol-powered chainsaws.

Types of defensive position

Infantry positions

The basic rifleman's position (*Schützenloch* – literally 'firing hole') was a two-man slit trench, analogous to a foxhole; it was also nicknamed a wolf's barrow (*Wolfgrabhügel*). While a one-man hole was used when necessary, the two-man was preferred. It offered soldiers moral support and allowed one to rest with the other on watch. Also, if a one-man position was knocked out, a wide gap was created in the defensive line, whereas in a two-man hole if one was lost the other could still conduct the defence. The one-man rifleman's position, nicknamed a 'Russian hole' (*Russenloch*), was a simple 70cm-wide, 60cm-deep hole – deep enough to allow a man to kneel in. Soil was piled in a crescent to the front to reduce the amount of digging required. As with other positions the soil was meant to be removed, but often time constraints meant the parapet remained. In the absence of a parapet, the rifle was propped on a small mound of earth or a Y-shaped fork driven into the ground. The 'Russian hole' could be deepened to allow a standing position and could later be widened for two men. Initially, two-man positions (*Schützenloch für 2 Gewehrschützen*) were specified as a short straight trench, 80cm by 1.8m. A slightly curved trench was also approved and this became standard in 1944. This version had two firing steps with a deeper centre section, allowing the riflemen to sit on the firing steps with their legs in the centre hole during shelling and offering protection from overrunning tanks. Armour protection trenches (*Panzerdeckungsloch*) used the same concept and they too were suitable as rifle positions. They could be V-, W-, or U-shaped, or a shallow crescent. The firing steps were recommended to be 1.4m deep and the deeper central portion 1.8–2m. All of these positions were recommended to be 60–80cm wide at the top and 40cm at the bottom. The recommended distance between positions was 10m, but this varied depending on the unit's assigned frontage, the terrain and vegetation.

Anti-armour rifles were placed in two-man positions. No special positions were provided for *Panzerfausts*, they could be fired from any open position with a few considerations. This rocket launcher was normally fired held under the arm, but it could be fired from the shoulder from a dug-in position. In the latter case the rear of the breech end had to be clear of any obstructions because of the 30m back-blast, meaning no rear parapet; nor could the breech-end be angled down too far. They could not be fired from within buildings unless from a very large room, such as a warehouse, with open doors and windows to relieve blast overpressure. The same restrictions applied to the 8.8cm *Panzerschreck*, but it had a greater back-blast. They were often employed in threes with two positioned forward and one to the rear, the distances dependent on terrain. This allowed the launchers to engage

Panzergrenadiers from the Grossdeutschland Division in a two-man rifle position. They have erected a parapet to their front, and have provided it with a loophole. 'Egg 39' and 'stick 29' hand grenades lie ready on the edge of the hole.

enemy tanks approaching from any direction plus provided an in-depth defence: at least two of the launchers could engage a tank. A 2m-long, V-shaped slit trench without parapet was used, with the two ends of the 'V' oriented away from the enemy. The gunner would occupy the arm of the 'V' that offered the best engagement of the target tank, and the assistant would load and take shelter from the back-blast in the other arm.

The squad's two-man light machine-gun position (*Schützenloch für leichte Maschinegewehr*), or 'machine-gun hole or nest' (*Maschine- gewehrloch oder nest*), was a slightly curved, 1.4–1.6m trench with two short armour protection trenches angled to the rear. On the forward side was a 20cm-deep U-shaped platform for the bipod-mounted gun. The position could be placed anywhere within the squad line that provided it the best field of fire. Alternate positions were meant to be up to 50m from the primary position, but were often closer. The three-man heavy machine-gun position (*Schützenloch für s.MG.*) was similar to the light one, but with armour protection trenches extending from the ends. The platform was still 20cm deep, requiring the long tripod legs to be dug in to lower the weapon's profile. The difference in design between the light and heavy positions was a weakness, as it allowed aerial photographic interpreters to differentiate between the types. A common design would have prevented this.

Expedient efforts and materials were used to construct positions. As the Soviets swept into East Prussia in late-1944, the Germans employed civilians to construct defensive positions and obstacles behind the field army, so that it could fall back on them. Two sections of 1.5m-diameter, 2m-long concrete culvert pipe were used to build 'Tobruk pit' machine-gun positions. A pit was dug and one section laid horizontally on the bottom with one end shored with sandbags or planks, creating the troop shelter. The second pipe was set vertically, with a U-shaped section cut out of one side of the bottom end to mate with the horizontal pipe. The top

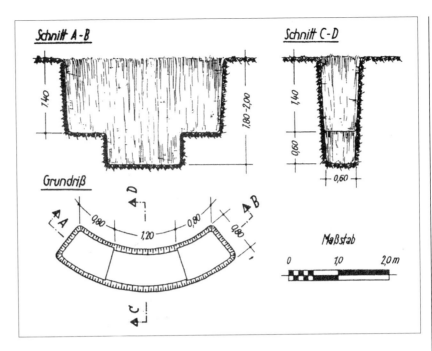

A curved-type *Schützenloch für 2 Schützen* (rifle position for two riflemen). These were also dug straight.

A heavy machine-gun position for a tripod-mounted gun could accommodate the two-man crew plus the squad leader.

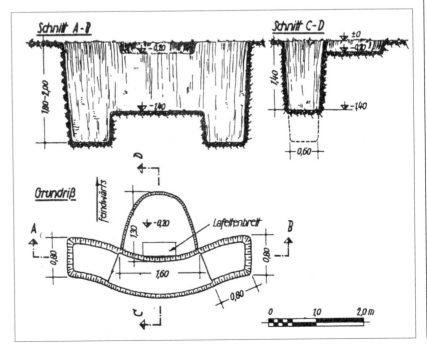

The light machine-gun position for a bipod-mounted gun could accommodate two men.

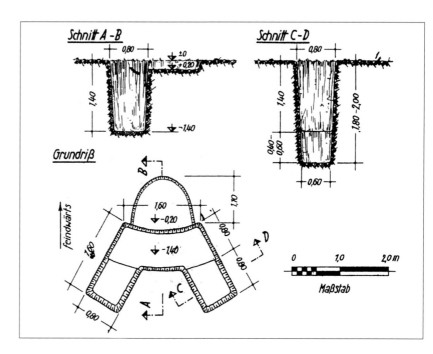

An 8.8cm *Panzerschreck* R.PzB.43 rocket-launcher position. This weapon was shoulder-fired and served in an anti-armour role. The end points of the 'V' (at the bottom of the photo) face away from the enemy. The gunner could fire from either arm of the trench, allowing him a flank shot on passing enemy tanks. The other one or two crewmen would shelter from the back-blast in the opposite arm. Note that the area to the rear is clear of obstructions and camouflage. Two or three (sometimes more) of these positions might cover a specific Allied armour avenue of approach.

end of the vertical pipe was flush with the ground. It was quick to build and easily camouflaged.

If a position was occupied for long enough, the rifle and machine-gun positions might be connected by trenches. Trench systems were widely used in the desert as they allowed concealed movement between firing positions in terrain otherwise devoid of cover. They were also used extensively within strongpoints. Trenches followed the terrain's contours in difference to the geometric patterns laid out in World War I-style that ignored the terrain. Trench systems were not necessarily continuous. Some sections may have been covered with branches and saplings and perhaps a light covering of earth or snow. Trench patterns were zig-zag with each section 10–15m in length: in this way, artillery or mortar rounds striking the trench would only inflict casualties in the section struck. The angled trench sections also prevented any enemy troops that gained the trench from firing down its full length. Crawl trenches (*Kriechgraben*) were 60–80cm wide at the top (as specified for all trenches), 60cm deep and 60cm wide at the bottom. Connecting trenches (*Verbingdungsgraben*) or approach trenches (*Annäherungsgraben*) were 1.8–2m deep and 40cm wide at the bottom. Battle trenches (*Kampfgraben*) were the same, but with firing steps (*Schützennische*) and ammunition niches cut into the sides. Some firing steps might be cut into the trench's rear side for all-round defence. Connecting trenches too might have firing steps, and adjoining armour protection trenches were recommended every 40–50m. Two-man rifle and machine-gun positions were usually dug 2–3m forward of the battle trench and connected by slit trenches (*Stichgraben*). These were located at the points of trench angles and along the straight sections. Dugout shelters (*Unterschlupfe*) protecting one to six men were situated in the trench's forward side at intervals, and nicknamed 'dwelling bunkers' (*Wohnbunker*). These provided protection from sudden artillery and air attacks and tank overruns. They were built as small as possible and in a variety of manners. As the position developed, squad and half-squad bunkers were built off connecting trenches for both protection from artillery and as living quarters. In muddy and wet conditions plank duckboards (*Lattenroste*) might be placed in the trench's bottom over a central drainage gutter.

Crew-served weapons positions

The 5cm mortar position (*Schützenloch für leicht Granatwerfer*) was a simple slit trench similar to a two-man rifle position, with a 70cm × 1m × 70cm step in the front for the mortar. Shallow rectangular pits were also dug as hasty positions with a U-shaped parapet open in the front. The pit for the 8cm heavy mortar (*Nest für s.Gw.*) was a 1.6m-deep circular pit, 1.8m in diameter at the bottom. The top would be slightly larger, the degree of side slope depending on the stability of the soil. A 1m³ shelf was cut in the back for ammunition. On either side were armour protection trenches.

In 1943 the '8cm heavy mortar pit' was redesignated the 'firing position for medium mortar' (*Feuerstellung für mittleren Granatwerfer*), as the new 12cm had been adopted as a heavy mortar. The latter's *Feuerstellung für s.Gw.* was simply an enlarged version of its 8cm counterpart, 2m deep and 2m in diameter. Since mortars were highly mobile and relatively small, they were often simply emplaced behind any available cover such as in gullies and ditches, or behind mounds, walls or rubble.

'Nests' for anti-armour and infantry guns too were redesignated 'firing positions' in 1943. Anti-armour gun positions were circular or oval, about 4m across (though this varied), and shallow (40cm for 3.7cm anti-armour guns, and slightly deeper for the 5cm and 7.5cm). Slots were sometimes dug for the wheels to lower the profile of these anti-armour guns. Infantry-gun positions were similar, but deeper (3m in diameter, 50cm deep for the 7.5cm; 6m in diameter, 1.3m deep for the 15cm). Ramps dug in the position's rear allowed the gun to be emplaced and withdrawn. A low parapet was placed some 2m behind the ramp's upper end to protect the position's rear opening. If armour protection trenches were not dug on either side of the position, shallow slit trenches were dug inside the position immediately adjacent to the gun and in some instances beneath the gun between the wheels. In fully developed positions a downward angled ramp was sometimes dug, and the gun could be rolled down this to place it below ground level. The lower end of the ramp was sometimes provided with overhead cover (*Untersellraum*). These were sometimes built for anti-armour and flak guns as well. Infantry guns, being smaller and lighter than artillery pieces, were often emplaced in hastily built positions, like mortars. Anti-armour guns by necessity had to be in well-concealed positions to

BELOW TOP A light machine-gun position with a small firing platform and no parapet. A communications trench at the top connects this position to other ones. The boards lying forward of the position prevented dust from giving away its location.

BELOW BOTTOM A light machine-gun position with a large firing platform and a niche for the ammunition bearer. The parapet is low in order to reduce the profile of the position. This practice was first adopted in the featureless landscape of North Africa and was later used in other open areas.

survive and inflict losses on enemy tanks. They also had to be able to relocate to other positions quickly once detected by the enemy. For this reason, while a gun's initial position may have been a fully prepared one, subsequent positions were often only partly prepared or simply a hastily selected site providing concealment and the necessary field of fire.

2cm flak guns, single and quad, were increasingly employed in forward positions in the ground fire role, especially on the Eastern Front. When deployed so, they were positioned on their own in the frontline. The firing position for 2cm flak (*Feuerstellung für 2cm Flak*) was circular, 5.5m in diameter and 45cm deep, and was lined with ammunition niches and compartments for gun equipment. 2cm and 3.7cm guns were set on a slightly elevated triangular platform.

The 8.8cm flak gun was sometimes employed as an *ad hoc* anti-armour gun on all fronts. While extremely accurate at long range and capable of knocking out any tank with high rates of fire, it had its limitations in this role. It was very large and had a high profile, making it difficult to conceal and requiring a great deal of effort to dig in. Its large size and the need for a heavy prime mover made it difficult and slow to withdraw and reposition. When used in the anti-armour role, the '88' was hidden among buildings, or in wooded areas, or defiladed in gullies and road cuts.

Divisional field artillery pieces were provided circular or roughly triangular firing positions (*Geschützestellung*). These usually had substantial all-round parapets and were deeper than other more forward gun positions for protection from counter-battery fire. Ready ammunition niches might be dug into the forward side, armour protection trenches attached to the sides, a rear entry/exit ramp added, and separate ammunition niches and crew shelters located to the rear. A simple artillery firing position was prepared by digging a shallow pit and piling the earth to the front. Any existing cover might be used for this purpose. Armour protection trenches or merely simple slit trenches were dug to either side of the gun to protect the crew from ground, artillery and air attack. As air attack became common, these slit trenches were placed further from the gun position. Several ammunition niches were dug to the rear. A battery's four gun positions were set 30–50m apart and could be placed in a straight or staggered line, a square or a diamond formation. The battery headquarters was to the rear of the positions. The horse and ammunition wagon parking was well to the rear of the battery position (up to 200m) in a concealed area to protect it from artillery. Camouflage was essential for the battery to survive, and so positions were often covered with camouflage nets. Each battery had two light machine guns for ground and air defence.

Slit trenches were dug in rear areas as air raid shelters (*Luftschutzraum*). These varied in form and dimension, but two typical examples were the straight trench (2m long, 40–60cm wide and 1.6m deep), and the three-leg zig-zag trench which had each leg with approximately the same dimensions as the straight trench. Trenches might be roofed over with earth-covered logs or bundled brushwood fascines. Interestingly, such shelters were dug in at distances as great as 40km behind the front.

Squad bunkers

A variety of different designs of squad and half-squad underground shelters or bunkers (*Gruppen und Halbgruppen-*

Flak positions

The Germans categorised flak gun positions according to their conditions of employment (*Feldmäßig*). (1) *Feldmäßig*: the gun was simply set up in the open and remained on the carriage. (2) *Feldmäßiger Ausbau*: the gun was dismounted from the carriage and positioned behind a hastily erected parapet (made of earth, sand, rocks, logs, sandbags, or packed snow). (3) *Verstärkter Feldmäßiger Ausbau*: a purpose-built position of planks and timber, brick, or light concrete. (4) *Ständiger Ausbau*: a solid, permanent, concrete position that included flak towers.

While the parapet's exterior shape and thickness could vary, the interior dimensions of a six-sided position are given below. Square-shaped positions with approximately the same cross-section measurements were also common.

Calibre	Cross-section A	Sidewall B
2–2.5cm	5m	2m
2cm (quad)–4cm	6m	2.5m
5cm–10.5cm	7m	3m
12.8cm	8m	4m

2cm and 3.7cm flak platoons were positioned with the three guns in a triangle, with the point facing the expected direction of air attack. The interval between the guns was 50–75m, reduced to 30m in 1944. From that time, rather than having the guns under the control of individual gun commanders, a single command post was situated in the position's centre.

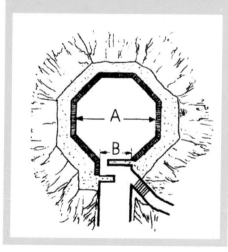

unterstand) were available for protection and living. These bunkers were built to the rear of the main defences, within strongpoints and near crew-served weapons positions. They were not fighting positions, being completely below ground and lacking firing ports. They were to provide more practical living quarters than small dugouts, trenches and holes. They also provided good protection from artillery and air attack, as well as the extremes of wind, rain, snow and cold. Wherever possible, they were built completely below ground level, with the top flush with the ground. If the water table or extremely hard or rocky ground prevented a buried bunker they were dug as deep as possible with double log walls (50cm between logs), filled with rock or packed soil, and the above-ground sides and roof banked with packed soil and covered with sod. Entry was gained through a trench (connected to a communications trench), down some stairs, and into a vestibule separated from the main room, although this last luxury was not always present. Wood floors were provided if sufficient dimensioned lumber was available. When it was not, straw was used, which had to be changed periodically. Individual or multi-person two- or three-level platform bunks (*Pritsche*) were integrated. A table (*Tisch*) and benches (*Bank*) were provided. Rifle racks (*Gewehrständer*) might be mounted on a wall near the door. Sometimes a short emergency exit tunnel was provided.

A squad trench in the final days of the war, in East Prussia. Firing steps have been cut into the trench's sides. In the upper centre is the entrance to a squad bunker.

If available a wood or oil stove (*Ofen*) was installed with a stovepipe. Small, canister-like, gasoline-burning heaters were used such as the motor vehicle heater and the smaller Juwel 33 heater. Little folding stoves (*Esbit Kocher*), fuelled by hexamethylene tetamine tablets, were used to heat mess tins. Sand-filled cans soaked with petrol were used for heat during cold nights. Light was provided by kerosene lanterns, candles (with melted wax remoulded into new candles) and small ration cans fitted with a wick burning rifle oil known as a 'Hindenburg lamp' (*Hindenburger Lampe*). Expended cartridge cases, 2cm or 3.7cm for example, had the mouth crimped to a narrow slit, filled with oil, and a wick inserted to make a crude lamp. Issue field pocket lamps (*Feldtaschen Lampe*, flashlights) were used sparingly as batteries were scarce.

The elaborate bunkers pictured in manuals could not always be built in urgent

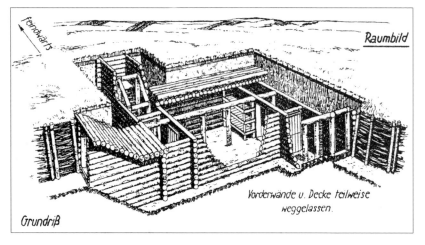

Squad (*Gruppenunterstand*) and half-squad bunkers (*Halbgruppenunterstand*) were built in many forms, from simple single rooms to large, complex, multi-room bunkers.

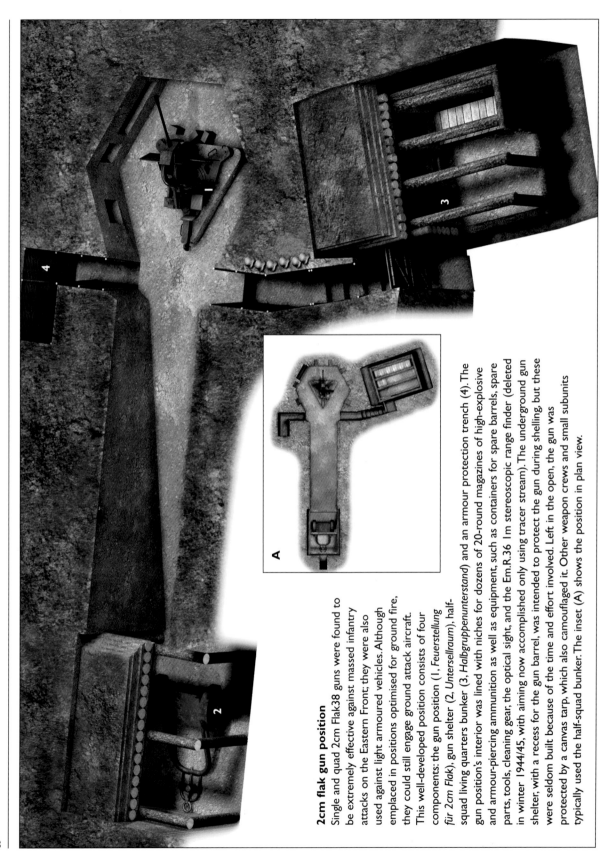

2cm flak gun position

Single and quad 2cm Flak38 guns were found to be extremely effective against massed infantry attacks on the Eastern Front; they were also used against light armoured vehicles. Although emplaced in positions optimised for ground fire, they could still engage ground attack aircraft. This well-developed position consists of four components: the gun position (1, *Feuerstellung für 2cm Flak*), gun shelter (2, *Untersellraum*), half-squad living quarters bunker (3, *Halbgruppenunterstand*) and an armour protection trench (4). The gun position's interior was lined with niches for dozens of 20-round magazines of high-explosive and armour-piercing ammunition as well as equipment, such as containers for spare barrels, spare parts, tools, cleaning gear, the optical sight, and the Em.R.36 1m stereoscopic range finder (deleted in winter 1944/45, with aiming now accomplished only using tracer stream). The underground gun shelter, with a recess for the gun barrel, was intended to protect the gun during shelling, but these were seldom built because of the time and effort involved. Left in the open, the gun was protected by a canvas tarp, which also camouflaged it. Other weapon crews and small subunits typically used the half-squad bunker. The inset (A) shows the position in plan view.

situations. During December 1941, 6.Panzer-Division, with its former tank crews fighting as infantry, was forced from a chain of villages within a forested area. It could either withdraw to another line of villages and possibly be enveloped, or it could establish a hasty defensive line in a temperature of −49°F without adequate shelter, which would mean death from exposure. During the previous few days' engagements on open terrain, daily casualties from frostbite had risen drastically to 800 per day. The division would soon lose its ability to function. The immediate construction of bunkers for both fighting and shelter was essential. The single corps and two divisional engineer battalions had only 40–60 men each and very little equipment. However, the division had recently received a large quantity of demolitions. The engineer battalion commanders were ordered to disregard the harsh weather conditions and blast multiple lines of craters in the solidly frozen ground along the specified battle line to shelter all combat units and reserves. The craters were sighted to provide mutual in-depth fire support. Each crater/bunker could hold 3–5 men. The engineers also mined approaches and built tank obstacles at three sites. The reserves and service troops packed down paths between the craters and to the rear, essentially snow communications trenches. They used readily available lumber and logs to cover the craters.

The blasting of the crater lines began the next morning. The enemy appeared to think the blasting was artillery fire and did not advance. The blasting was completed by noon and by night the craters were finished by infantrymen with hand tools, covered with lumber, logs and snow, and occupied. Smoke soon rose from the bunkers, where the troops kept warm with open fires. Outposts were established forward of the bunkers, and abatis obstacles were laid in front of these, with anti-armour guns emplaced on higher ground covering the tank obstacles. The entire line was prepared within 12 hours of the first detonation. The engineers who prepared the positions suffered 40 per cent frostbite casualties, but the next day division frostbite casualties dropped from 800 to four. The line withstood all enemy attacks and was not abandoned until ten days later, in milder weather, when the adjacent units on both flanks were forced to withdraw after enemy tanks had penetrated their lines.

Principles of camouflage

German camouflage (*Tarnung*) practices attempted to blend fortifications into the surrounding terrain and vegetation to prevent detection from both the ground and air. Efforts were made to hide positions outright as well, an example being the completely buried below ground personnel bunkers. Natural materials were used alongside camouflage nets, screens and pattern painting. German directives stated that cover and camouflage measures should not obstruct a weapon's field of fire.

Basic camouflage principles of frontline positions included positioning emplacements within vegetated areas and among rubble and broken terrain, avoiding a neat orderly appearance (though manuals depicted fortifications as tidy, in practice they were not), avoidance of silhouetting against the sky and contrasting backgrounds, removing spoil or concealing turned earth, concealing firing ports with tree branches or wreckage materials, building fortifications inside existing buildings, and the fabrication of screens from brushwood to mask movement along roads and tracks. The dispersal of fortifications, positions and facilities in irregular patterns was also common.

In barren, snow-covered, and featureless desert areas it was cautioned that camouflaged positions should not be located near any existing features, otherwise this would allow an enemy observer to reference the position's location. Snow positions were not as easy to camouflage as may be assumed.

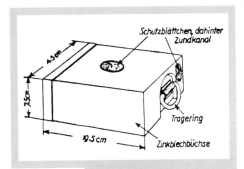

Blasting holes

Exceedingly hard, rocky or frozen ground proved to be virtually impossible to dig into with infantry hand tools. Blasting with TNT or picric acid demolition charges (*Sprengstoff*) was necessary. The cylindrical 100g boring cartridge 1928 (*Bohrpatrone 28*) was covered with light brown paper. The rectangular 200g demolition charge 1928 (*Sprengkörper 28*) was covered in brown paper, but picric acid charges were also issued with brown Bakelite covers. The 1kg demolition charge 1924 (*Sprengbüchse 24*) had a green, rectangular pressure-resistant zinc casing, which allowed it to be used under water. There were also 3kg (pictured above) and 10kg (6.6 lb and 22 lb) charges similar to the 1kg. A starter hole was dug by hand and a small charge inserted. The explosion created a small crater in which progressively larger charges were detonated until a hole of the desired size was obtained. German pioneers possessed earth-boring drills; if these were available, a deep hole could be made and a large charge inserted, creating a sizeable crater. Loose spoil was then removed from the hole, the interior squared off, and firing steps and ammunition niches added.

A four-metre Em.R.4m range-finder used with 8.8cm flak guns in an above ground position. This is an excellent example of small-diameter log revetting banked with earth on the exterior. The earth banking has been covered with camouflaging sods. The entrance to the right has been revetted with planks of wood.

An incomplete tank turret emplacement (*Ringstand für Panzerkampfwagen Turn*), here using a 7.5cm Panther Pz.Kpfw.V turret. The turret was mounted on a steel frame and could be hand-traversed. The frame's sides would be strengthened with timbers or logs and banked with earth. Beneath the frame is the crew's log-built shelter. While under construction, the position was camouflaged from aerial detection by branches, which have been pulled away to allow it to be photographed.

Dug-up snow looks very different to undisrupted snow and even after additional snowfall it appears different. Vehicle and foot tracks point to positions. Machine guns cause black powder marks in front of firing ports making them easy to detect. Any movement, even by white-clad troops, is easily detectable against snow backgrounds. Smoke from heating and cooking fires also signals the locations of positions. White sheets were often used to conceal crew-served weapons, but were easily detected at close range.

The removal of soil from around positions and the lack of parapets were for concealment purposes. It is extremely difficult to detect such positions from ground level, especially if all signs of work have been removed or concealed. Soil parapets around positions are easily detectable from the air because of the turned soil's contrast with surrounding undisturbed soil and vegetation, which appears white or very light grey. Parapets also cast shadows, which are detectable from the air. The lack of parapets for concealment was especially effective in the desert and Russian steppes.

One determining factor might be the location of a position in relation to enemy ground-level observers. A parapet might be thrown up behind a position so that the occupants would not be silhouetted against the sky or contrasting terrain. When parapets were built they were sometimes camouflaged with sod removed from the position's site and beneath where the parapets would be thrown. The soil was spread outward from the position and the parapet kept low. Evergreen tree branches were also used to conceal parapets, but had to be replaced every couple of days: in the Russian winter they froze and remained green for some time. If the ground was covered with fallen leaves these too were spread over parapets and other turned soil for camouflage. Positions were often placed on the reserve slopes of hills and ridges to conceal them from ground observation and direct fire. Camouflage nets were used to conceal the entrances to bunkers, erected over artillery positions, and sometimes laid on the ground to cover trenches and their parapets. In the latter case the nets were supported by taut wire staked in a zig-zag pattern over the trench, and it also supported camouflaging brush and branches.

Riflemen's positions were sometimes camouflaged with camouflage tent quarters (*Zeltbahn* rain capes), covers woven from vines and twigs, and sections cut from camouflage nets. Lift-up lids for riflemen's positions were made by constructing a criss-crossed stick frame and wiring on sections of sod trimmed to match the surrounding ground. These are known as 'spider holes'.

The use of dummy positions and facilities and mock-up vehicles was very common, especially in Africa. Since it was impossible to conceal activity in the desert, deception efforts were widespread. To be effective, dummy vehicles had to be moved nightly, at least partly camouflaged, and fake tracks had to be made. Dummy bunkers were constructed by simply piling, shaping, and lightly camouflaging spoil removed from actual positions, which provided a means of disposing of excess soil. Knee-deep dummy trenches connected dummy positions and were filled with brush to make them appear deeper from the air. Sentries manned dummy positions and fires were burned to make them appear occupied.

This U-shaped 10.5cm 18/1 Wespe ('wasp') self-propelled howitzer position was also used to shelter tanks and assault guns. It might be used as a firing position or as a shelter for protection from artillery and air attack. Such emplacements were commonly built into hedgerows or hidden beneath trees, and were also dug deeper without a parapet, with only the turret exposed above ground level. The crew would often dig a shallow pit beneath the vehicle to sleep in.

Any night-time illumination can sharply silhouette a defensive position, as demonstrated here by the muzzle flash of a mortar.

Theatre-specific defences

North Africa

When the advance elements of the Afrikakorps arrived at Tripoli in February 1941 they found the Libyan Desert to be a totally alien environment. Regardless of the much-touted preparatory training that the troops bound for Africa received they were ill prepared.

Most of the fighting in Libya and Egypt occurred on the coastal strip extending up to 60km inland. This region predominantly comprises undulating ground crossed by 4–20m high ridges and hills with gentle slopes. The high ground is covered with barren exposed rock, much of it loose. In the wide flat valleys the rocky ground is covered by chalk, clay and dust on which patches of camel thorn grow. Wet and dry salt marshes are dotted along the coast. In some areas broad *wadis* cut the ground. These were normally dry watercourses edged by low banks, broken in many areas allowing vehicle passage, and with sand bottoms. The areas referred to as mountains are only a few hundred metres above sea level, and are barren, rocky, terraced and cut by numerous gouges and ravines. Sand dunes were encountered along the coast, at the base of the 'mountain ranges', near large *wadis*, and in the desert proper inland from the coastal plain.

Every metre of elevation provided an advantage for both observation, fields of fire, and cover. The lack of vegetation and significant high ground in most areas made camouflage efforts a challenge. *Wadis* were something of an obstacle, but were valuable for concealing units, vehicles and positions, as were the reverse slopes of low ridges.

The chalk surface found on much of the coastal plain presented both problems and advantages for the construction of field works. This layer was formed when winter rains were absorbed and then rose to the surface in the summer: their evaporation created a hard cement-like crust of gravel and dissolved chalk and silica. This surface crust could be 50cm–2m thick within 30km of the coast, lessening in thickness and firmness further inland and diminishing in the deep desert. A major effort was required to dig though the chalk layer, and often required blasting or power tools. Beneath it was soft soil or sand. Often a small hole was cut through the chalk and chambers dug out beneath it. The 1–2m-thick overhead chalk layer did not require support for distances up

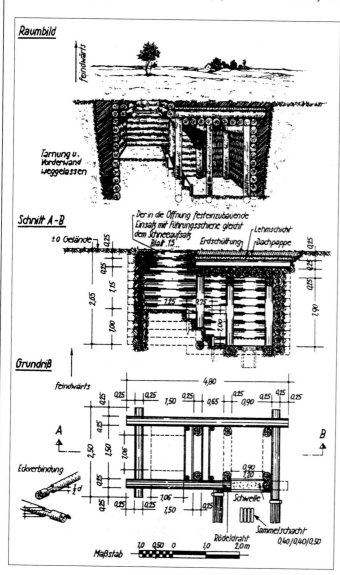

A Tobruk light machine-gun position built from logs rather than the usual concrete (*Machinegewehr-Ringstand aus Rundholz*). The overhead cover was always flush with the ground, making the position difficult to detect. Note the inset illustration at the bottom left showing the method of notching logs.

to 35m and was able to resist bombardment. Soft sidewalls had to be revetted. Dried-up cisterns, called *Bir*, dating from Roman times, were used as command posts, shelters and ammunition points. These had a small influx hole through the chalk layer and consisted of roughly 10m × 10m chambers.

The lack of wood meant that sandbags (in short supply), rocks, sand-filled ammunition boxes and petrol tins were extensively used for revetting. When positions could not be dug in the hard chalk layer, rocks were simply stacked in low circular walls creating a *sangar* (a Kashmiri term widely adopted by the British) – the German term was *In Felsen gehauene* (rock-encased). Unless made to appear like a natural rock pile, they were easy to detect at moderate ranges. Since materials to construct overhead cover were not available, positions would be dug into the ground in the thinner surface chalk areas and then niches dug at right angles beneath the crust layer. Even in the chalk-surface areas, loam and clay-filled depressions and *wadi* bottoms allowed positions to be dug as normal. In coastal areas brackish water was found within 1m of the surface, forcing shallow, partly above-ground positions to be built. In the rear areas spoil would be heaped in parapets. Tents and shelter quarters were pitched in pits and over slit trenches so the occupants slept below ground level and had protection from the sun and nighttime cold. In the frontline and outpost positions, soil was to be removed and parapets not used. This made it extremely difficult to detect fighting positions from even short ranges. If spoil could not be removed it was spread out around the position to a height of no more than 22cm. This usually created a layer of contrasting soil though. Desert haze, dust and ground glare all served to further conceal positions dug into the ground at longer ranges. In areas with hard or rocky ground the positions were shallow, forcing the defenders to remain motionless all day under the blistering heat and swarming flies, with many suffering from dysentery.

Camouflage of positions and vehicles was impossible in most areas. Dust clouds and vehicle tracks made it even more difficult. Once a weapon had been fired, its position was revealed by dust. *Wadis*, depressions and reverse slopes were used to the maximum extent possible. Camouflage nets and camel thorn were used to conceal vehicles. This may not have totally hidden the vehicle, but it prevented its distinctive shadow from revealing its presence and type. Key vehicles were dug in if possible and widely dispersed.

Barbed-wire and man-made obstacles in general were little used because of the lack of materials, the wide frontages and the capacity to outflank positions. They were sometimes employed around strongpoints though, but from the air they highlighted the positions they protected. When used they were often placed on low ground or reverse slopes. Barbed wire was more effective concealed if 200m from the frontline than 50m and exposed in the open. Extensive anti-armour and anti-personnel minefields were relied on as the principal obstacle.

Attempts were initially made to emulate European defensive zones with near continuous lines. This proved ineffective and a strongpoint system was developed. Often each squad established a strongpoint with support weapons distributed to them. The squad strongpoint would have its light machine gun plus possibly a heavy machine gun, anti-armour or 2cm flak gun, and sometimes a mortar, with all positions connected by trenches. Two squads would be forward and one back. Platoons and companies would similarly be deployed in what was called a 'chequered' defence area in at least three lines and to a depth of at least 200m. Depth was critical, and preferred to a solid, continuous front. Fire and mines covered the gaps between strongpoints. Often efforts were made to link all the strongpoints with connecting trenches. This was acceptable within platoon areas, but attempting to connect all strongpoints over large areas was a waste of time, effort and resources. Once the enemy attacked, troops remained in their strongpoints. Evacuation of casualties, ammunition resupply and redistribution of troops would not occur while directly engaged, only during lulls. The connecting trenches could not be defended and if the enemy gained them they provided him with covered approaches to the strongpoints.

Mobile units employed defensive tactics as well. When they halted for the night they would form a tight perimeter (*Lager*) on defendable, slightly elevated ground with clear fields of fire: all tank guns, artillery pieces and anti-armour guns would be placed in the perimeter and soft-skin transport vehicles in the centre. Infantry would establish outposts on possible approaches. While mobile warfare was preferred in the desert, German offensives could not be sustained and the defence assumed great importance as Allied strength grew in North Africa.

Italy

The Apennine Mountains spread along almost the entire length of the Italian Peninsula. Rivers running into the sea across the hilly coastal plains cross-compartment the peninsula with narrow, flat valleys. The valleys were extremely muddy in the winter and spring. A force fighting its way up the peninsula was faced with repetitive ridges and steep-sided mountains. Citrus and olive groves and vineyards covered the terraced lower slopes and evergreen and scrub trees the upper. The roads were few and very restrictive being limited to valleys with only infrequent passes. The ground was extremely rocky. Villages were situated on naturally dominating terrain making them ideal for defence as well as shelter from the harsh weather. The thick-walled buildings, most with cellars, were substantially constructed of stone and mortar and the towns irregularly arranged. They provided even better defensive positions when rubbled. Anti-armour and machine guns were often emplaced in cellars and the overhead floors reinforced by rubble. AFVs were limited to the easily blocked narrow roads and were extremely exposed when approaching towns.

In many areas the terrain was cut by so many intertwined ridges, ridge fingers, gorges and ravines that not all approaches could be defended. The bases and lower slopes of mountains were often covered with jumbled boulders

This Italian-designed, hexagonal pillbox, featuring multiple machine-gun ports, was extensively used by the Germans in Italy. Some were better camouflaged than others, blending in well with the rocky terrain. However, because the embrasures were rock-faced, machine gun fire directed into them would ricochet into the pillbox, creating rock fragments.

and loose rocks. Attackers, if they had effectively reconnoitered, would infiltrate the defended area and even attack it from above, the rear or the flank. While mutual support between fighting positions was desired, what Field Marshall Albert Kesselring called a 'string of pearls', the terrain was often too rough and too many positions were required to block every avenue of approach. Anti-personnel mines were used extensively and anti-tank mines could easily block roads, as did demolitions. While the mountains and ridges provided the defender with excellent long-range observation (clouds, fog, rain and snow permitting), fields of fire and observation in the immediate vicinity of defensive positions were usually limited. Surprise attacks and close-range fights were common.

Abundantly available rock was the most commonly used construction material for pillboxes, bunkers and other positions. Cement was sometimes available for mortar allowing substantial structures to be built. Railroad ties and rails were also available. In the well-prepared, in-depth defensive lines, such as the Gustav Line spanning the peninsula south-east of Rome, concrete fortifications were built. Rock-built fortifications hidden among the scrub trees were easily blended into the surrounding terrain and difficult to detect from the ground or air.

The 160km Gustav Line had been established along the Rapidi and Sangro river valleys in the autumn of 1943. Mountains in this area ranged from 900m to over 2,200m high. The Germans were able to maintain an adequate mobile reserve on the Italian Front. An outer defence line, the Winter Line, protected its western half. When this and the western Gustav Line were penetrated, the Germans fell back, hinging on 1,533m Monte Cassino, and established the *Führer Riegel*, known to the Allies as the Hitler Line, while the eastern portion of the Gustav Line remained intact until broken in mid-1944. (*Riegel* means 'bar' as in 'a bar on the door'. It was renamed *Senger Riegel*, after the commander of XIV Panzer-Korps, to avoid having a 'defeat' line named after the Führer.)

Since digging was difficult to impossible, defenders made use of ravines, gullies, knolls and ground folds. Blasting was required to excavate many positions. There were usually enough nooks and crannies that could be covered over with logs and topped by rock for suitable fighting positions and shelters, if they were in the necessary location to cover approaches. Rock *sangars* were extensively used and these too were sometimes covered. Mortars proved to be especially effective in the short-range battles as they could respond quickly and their steep trajectory allowed them to reach into ravines and behind steep ridges.

The Eastern Front

The Soviet Union provided a wide variety of terrain, including immense forests, huge wooded swamps, vast seemingly endless steppes and mountains. Each of these areas presented its own challenges and opportunities to the Germans in defence.

Forests allow only limited fields of observation and fire to both the defender and attacker. The advantages to the defenders are the limited and channelled AFV approaches, ease of concealment from ground and air observation, and abundant building and obstacle materials. The Germans would not defend on the forward edge of a forest, but would dig in well within the forest to make the enemy guess their location, make it difficult to adjust artillery fire on them, and avoid direct fire from the approaching enemy. Outposts (to warn of the enemy's approach) and observers (to direct artillery) were positioned on the wood line. Heavy timber roadblocks were constructed and abitis obstacles made from fallen trees, and tangled branches provided good anti-personnel obstacles. They could restrict fields of fire and observation though, as did dense vegetation, forcing positions to be located more closely together. Fields of fire in forests were not stripped bare as this would alert the enemy. Small bushes

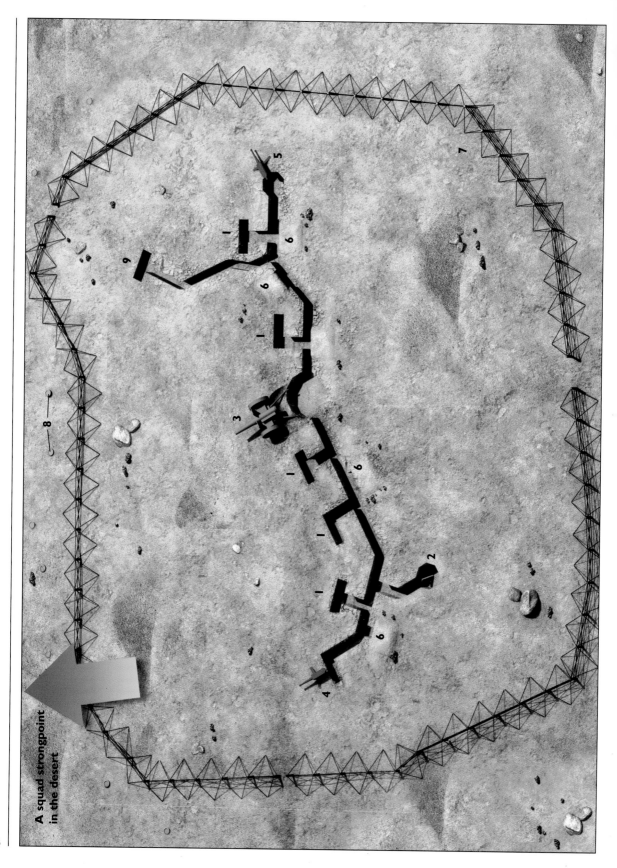

A squad strongpoint
in the desert

A squad strongpoint in the desert

Because of the need to defend wide frontages in the desert and the expansive fields of observation and fire, German units often built self-contained, widely scattered, reinforced squad strongpoints. An ideal example is shown here. The weapons positions and dugouts were to be at least 6m apart along the 40–60m zig-zag trench. One- and two-man rifle positions (1) were set 1–2m forward of the trench. Firing steps might be used, including on the trench's rear side. Not all such strongpoints had an 8cm mortar (2). A 2cm flak gun may have been substituted for the 3.7cm or 5cm anti-armour gun (3, shown above scale for clarity). Some strongpoints may have had two machine guns, one at each end (4 and 5). Lacking a flak gun, one of the machine guns (5) would be provided with an air-defence mount as well as an alternative position for ground fire. This combination of weapons provided the strongpoint with direct and indirect anti-personnel fire, direct anti-armour fire and air defence. Sufficient dugouts and small bunkers (6, hidden) were available for all personnel. Such a strongpoint might be manned by 16–24 troops. It would be sighted on any piece of high ground, even if only a couple of metres above the surrounding desert. Camouflage nets might have been used. The barbed-wire barrier (7), if present, was erected c. 50m from the strongpoint. Anti-armour mines would be emplaced outside the barbed wire along with some anti-personnel mines (8). The listening post (9), accessed via a crawl trench, was manned at night to guard against infiltration. Flare pistols were used to signal other strongpoints and command posts that a strongpoint was under attack, with coloured flare combinations identifying the type of attack and direction. The large red arrow (*feindwärts*) indicates the direction towards the enemy.

and lower branches were selectively removed and the bare cut marks smeared with mud so that the enemy unknowingly entered the field of fire. Individual riflemen, snipers and machine gunners could be scattered in-depth to make forward movement of the enemy difficult. They also protected gaps between units. Anti-armour guns could be concentrated and placed in-depth along the few roads penetrating the forest. Indirect fire weapons had to be positioned where scarce clearings provided high-angle fire rather than being positioned to optimise their range.

Swamps had characteristics similar to forests, but caused severe problems for both defender and attacker. The flooded terrain, though shallow, severely limited movement and made large attacks difficult. To the defender's advantage was the fact that AFVs could seldom be employed. The few dirt roads and tracks could not support armour. It also made the supply of forward positions and the movement of heavy weapons difficult. Every patch of above-water ground and every clump of trees were used for defensive positions. High-water tables meant most positions had to be built above ground. Timber fighting positions were built on log rafts and could be moved to better positions if required. Mines could not generally be used.

On the Russian steppes, long snow-bank barriers formed defensive lines with firing positions. Dugouts too were set in the snow berms, which were revetted with snow-filled fuel drums and hay bails (as shown here). Canvas tarps sometimes covered the dugout entrances.

Pakfront

The Germans developed the *Pakfront* (armour defence gun front) concept in Russia in 1943. This was an extension of the idea of emplacing anti-armour guns behind the forward positions and engaging them after the enemy had broken through, the reasoning being that the enemy was in a more disorganised state at this point, with its armour separated from any supporting infantry. Soviet armour usually broke through in large numbers, and since some at least remained under the effective control of the commander, they could drive into the German rear and cause havoc. The concept called for the divisional anti-armour battalion (corps- and army-level battalions were also employed) to position 6–10 (sometimes more) 7.5cm anti-armour guns (pictured below to the rear of the 3.7cm and 5cm) under a single commander on favourable terrain that blocked the main tank routes into the rear. The guns were well dug in and concealed. Their prime movers were hidden close by to quickly relocate the guns to alternative positions or a second fallback *Pakfront* position. In effect the *Pakfront* ambushed marauding tanks at short range with all guns opening fire simultaneously. Artillery and rocket projector (*Nebelwerfer*) fire would support the *Pakfront* as available reserves and armour moved into counter-attack positions. The Soviets adopted a similar anti-tank reserve (*Protivotankovny Rezerv*).

ABOVE The view from an Eastern Front trench. The irregular piles on the berm served as camouflage. Beyond the trench is a battered barbed-wire cattle fence reinforced with tangled brush.

The hundreds of kilometres of broad, gently rolling steppes were barren terrain, with few roads, villages, rivers or notable features. It was often impossible for units to determine their location on a map, as the sunflower-covered land was flat from horizon to horizon in all directions. There were fewer significant terrain features on which to defend than in the desert and fewer building materials. Simply digging in was all that could be accomplished. Units were often scattered widely with little contact between them. Whether defending or when halted during an advance, they prepared an all-round defence.

The fortifications at war

A battalion-level defence, early war

To examine the conduct of a doctrinal early-war defence, the battalion level is the most useful to look at. The deployment of the companies and platoons, the key defensive subunits, and the allocation and employment of battalion and regimental support weapons can be best scrutinised at this level. The later strongpoint defence and other methods of defending were simply modifications of this basic doctrine. The Germans viewed battalions as the building block of a formation's combat power. Regardless of how a unit was organised or what its reduced actual strength was, the number of battalions a division was able to field determined how it would be organised for combat and fight.

A battalion deployed two companies forward on its 800–2,000m front on defendable terrain with good fields of observation and fire. The third company was 100–300m to the rear, preferably too on defendable terrain, but also in a position from which to conduct an immediate counter-attack (*Gegenstoss*) in the event that the forward companies were pushed back. If the forward positions were penetrated and still partially intact, then the reserve company would serve as a blocking force (*Sperrverband*) to halt enemy penetrations or by manoeuvering into another position. The reserve company could also be manoeuvred to protect a flank if an adjacent battalion was penetrated or forced to withdraw.

A variety of support facilities were established in the battalion and company areas: command posts, ammunition points, medical aid posts, telephone exchanges, artillery observation posts, truck and wagon parks, and kitchen trailer positions.

Rifle platoons were positioned with their squads in relatively close proximity with narrow gaps between them; this was called a platoon point (*Zugspitze*). Three-squad platoons usually had all three squads on-line while four-squad platoons usually placed one to the rear covering the forward squads. In effect, each platoon position was a strongpoint and ideally would be partly surrounded by barbed wire and mines. Gaps between platoons and companies

The shadowy figure of a sentry stands guard over a canvas-wrapped machine-gun post. The position has been revetted with hay bails. Even though they were open-topped, these bails helped insulate the position.

were wider, but covered by patrols, fire, and, if time and resources allowed, mines. Some rifleman and machine-gun positions might be located outside the immediate platoon perimeter to cover gaps and approaches that could not be covered from within the position.

Each company deployed its reserve platoon several hundred metres forward in a widely scattered line across the company's sector. These were simple, hastily built positions serving to prevent surprise attacks, keep enemy patrols at bay, send out their own patrols, and warn of the enemy's approach. The outpost positions were sometimes situated to

make the enemy believe that this was a mainline or to mislead him into thinking the mainline was in a different direction. They would not attempt to conduct a stout resistance, but engage the enemy at long range and withdraw by concealed routes to the reserve position, which (if time allowed) had been prepared in advance.

It was found that artillery barrages and engineers easily penetrated continuous minefield belts laid across the front. Though dense mine belts were still employed on the Eastern Front and in North Africa, it was more effective to lay them within the main battle positions and at key points on roads, such as intersections and blockage points where off-road movement was restricted.

Field telephone lines were run down to platoon command posts and heavily relied on for communications. Radios were little used within battalions. Telephone lines were laid down gullies and roadside ditches, and time permitting, buried, to protect them from artillery and tracked vehicles. Messengers and signal pistols with coloured flares and smoke cartridges were also important means of communications.

The normal allocation of support weapons saw the regiment's two light infantry gun platoons each attached to a forward battalion; the heavy platoon remained under regimental control. The four regimental anti-armour company platoons gave the commander a great deal of flexibility: two platoons each to the two forward battalions, one platoon per forward battalion and two in reserve, one platoon per battalion with the fourth in the combat outpost position or protecting a flank are just some examples. With a platoon attached to a battalion usually two guns were detailed to each of its forward companies, but they may have been positioned behind the forward platoons. Alternate positions were prepared for each gun. Anti-armour weapons were often sited to enable them to engage tanks from the flank. The battalion machine-gun company's three platoons could be attached to each rifle company, or rather than one being attached to the reserve company, it could be under battalion control to secure a flank or in the combat outpost position. In forests and urban areas the heavy machine guns were often employed as light guns and deployed well forward with the rifle platoons to augment their close-range fire. Alternate positions were prepared for most machine guns. The mortar platoon's six mortars were usually retained under battalion control, but a mortar squad (two mortars) or a single mortar could be attached to each rifle company, which was the case with the strongpoint defence. The rifle company's three anti-armour rifles could be attached to each rifle platoon or grouped together as one element for volley fire against tanks.

The positioning of anti-armour guns and the sectors of fire they covered was based on the assessment of terrain over which enemy AFVs could approach. Terrain was classified as armour-proof (*Panzerschier*) – impassable to AFVs; armour-risk (*Panzergefährdet*) – difficult for tanks; or armour-feasible (*Panzermöglich*) – passable to armour. This determination was made by map and

Key to symbols:

▬ Anti-armour ditch

🚩 Btn command post

⌐ Coy command post

♦ Heavy machine gun

↑ Infantry gun

↥ Light anti-armour gun

● Light machine gun

⬤ Minefield

m∠ 8cm medium mortar

▲ Observation post

✳ Roadblock

Infantry battalion defence sector

A full-strength infantry battalion normally deployed for defence with two companies forward on its 800–2,000m front. The positions of the heavy machine guns and mortars of the battalion machine-gun company (4th) are depicted along with the four 3.7cm anti-armour guns and two 7.5cm infantry guns attached from the regiment. Each platoon position (*Zugspitze*) contains three light machine guns and a 5cm mortar. Medical posts and ammunition points are located near each company command post. In this instance the 1st Company on the left has two platoons (1/1 and 2/1) deployed on the main battle line (*Hauptkampflinie*) with the 3rd Platoon (3/1) in outposts (*Vorposten*). It would

withdraw to a reserve position behind 1/1 and 2/1 blocking the main road through the company sector. The 2nd Company on the right has its 3rd Platoon (3/2) also in an outpost position. It, however, would withdraw to a position on key terrain forward of 1/2 and 2/2. When forced to withdraw from that position it would occupy a reverse slope reserve position behind 1/2 and 2/2. The 3rd Company is positioned as the battalion reserve across the rear area. It can remain in position to block a breakthrough or conduct counter-attacks. The regimental boundary is shown by the 'III' line; the battalion boundary by the 'II' line; and the company boundary by the 'I' line. Contour lines for the terrain are also provided.

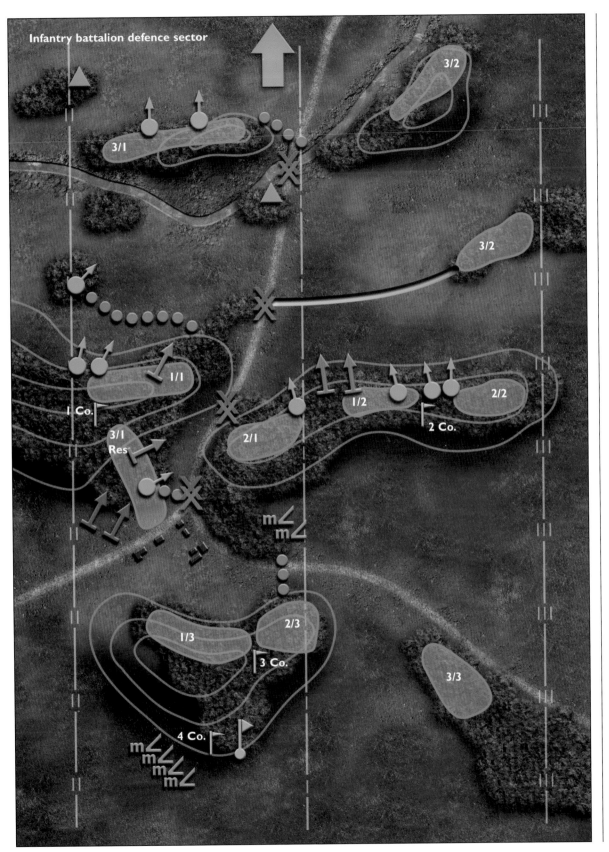

Infantry battalion defence sector

3/2

3/1

3/2

1/1

1 Co.

3/1
Res

2/1

1/2

2 Co.

2/2

m
m

1/3

2/3

3 Co.

3/3

4 Co.

m
m
m
m

ground reconnaissance. *Panzerschier* terrain included dense forests, swamps, marshes, deep mud, numerous large rocks and gullies, steep slopes, railroad embankments or cuts, etc. Infantry on the other hand might attack across such ground requiring it to be covered by machine guns and mortars.

Weapons engaged the enemy at much closer ranges than their maximum effective ranges. Some anti-armour guns would open fire at ranges up to 1,000m, but most would hold their fire until 150–300m. Anti-armour rifles engaged at the same range. Heavy infantry guns and mortars fired smoke rounds approximately one-third of the way back from the front of the attacking formation's lead tanks. This blinded the following vehicles, but did not screen the lead tanks from anti-armour gunners. The *Panzerfaust* had only 30, 60, and 100m ranges depending on the model, but tanks were engaged at much closer ranges to ensure a hit. The *Panzerschreck* usually engaged within 100m. Mortar and infantry gun concentrations were planned in front of and to the flanks of platoon and company positions, in the gaps between positions, in areas from which the enemy might attack, and in locations where he might emplace his own mortars. The infantry guns, possessing longer range than mortars, would be assigned deeper targets.

Early doctrine called for large-scale counter-attacks to be organised and launched, but this gave the enemy valuable time to consolidate on the objective and prepare to beat off the attack. Instead, counter-attacks were to be conducted as soon as possible on penetrating enemy forces in order to keep them off balance and delay their consolidating on the objective. Any unit in position launched squad or platoon attacks, rather than waiting for larger counter-attacks to be organised.

An Afrikakorps soldier attempts to create a hole in the crusty chalk gravel on a coastal plain. Blasting was often required, and piled rocks were used for cover.

El Alamein, Egypt, 1942

In September 1942 Rommel's offensive ground to a halt at Alam Halfa against stiff Commonwealth resistance. Having lost large numbers of AFVs and short of fuel, he chose to establish a strong defensive line rather than withdraw and lose the territory he had gained at great cost. He possessed sufficient mobile forces to halt British attacks with immediate counter-attacks. He did not possess enough for the mobile defence he preferred, and so would have to rely on a static, in-depth infantry defence.

A 61km-long defence zone was established from the coast 4km west of El Alamein south to the deep Qattara Depression providing a protected flank. The terrain was mostly flat, stoney desert with a few scattered ridges that became key positions. Some barbed wire was used, but the Germans relied on deeper, denser minefields than previously used. Existing British minefields were integrated into the German's two main belts, Minefields I and H, the 'Devil's Gardens' (*Teufelergarten*). Of the 445,000 mines laid, only three per cent were anti-personnel, lessening the danger to sappers breaching the fields.

Small observation and listening posts were established beyond the minefields to prevent infiltration by patrols. Within the western portion of Minefield I each infantry battalion positioned a company in the combat outpost line. Withdrawal lanes were provided through the fields. This zone was much thinner than normal and the British noted it during the offensive, having expected more resistance during the penetration of this area. The battalions' other two companies were in the main battle line with the bulk of the 800 anti-armour guns 1,000–2,000m behind the combat outposts and protected by Minefield H. The mine belts were compartmented and connected by traversing mine belts. With six weeks to prepare, the infantry defences were well developed and adequately protected from the near World War I-intensity artillery barrages. Some German units were mixed among the Italians in the line rather than placing the worse led and poorly armed units in their own sectors. The Italians provided the bulk of the infantry though with five infantry divisions in the line and only one German. This occurred too in the mobile reserve with a Panzer division paired with an Italian mobile division. The mobile reserves were positioned 1–3km behind the main battle line. This placed them within range of British artillery, countered by wide dispersal and digging in, but ensured their deployment rather than moving forward to counter-attack under air attack. A German and an Italian motorised infantry division were positioned astride the coastal highway 5–8km behind the front.

The Eighth Army attacked on the night of 23 October supported by massive artillery and air support. Sappers, after much effort, breached the minefields in the north. A supporting armour attack in the centre was repulsed, as was a larger attack in the south on the 25th. The British, with twice as many tanks as the Germans and Italians, broke out on 4 November. It had taken the much superior Commonwealth forces 12 days of intense close combat to break through a 3km-deep defence belt. Rommel, short of fuel and ammunition, having lost much of his armour, artillery and many anti-armour guns, successfully withdrew west as the British became bogged down in torrential rains.

Ortona, Italy, December 1943

The Germans were adept at defending towns and those in Italy were especially suitable for defence, with their heavily constructed stone and concrete multi-storey buildings with cellars. Combat in built-up areas was costly to both the defender and attacker. The Germans made the seizure of towns as punishing as possible for the Allies and took advantage of the cover and concealment towns provided from artillery and air and the time it bought. Ortona was to be the first town in which the Germans conducted a major defensive and delaying effort.

To the Germans a town was a ready-built strongpoint and a deathtrap for enemy tanks. The main defence line was located well within the town to deny the enemy observation and direct artillery and tank fire on the defences. Outposts and observation posts were placed on the town's edge with others well outside the town to observe avenues of approach. Mines and other obstacles blocked roads, bridges were demolished, and mines and anti-armour ditches were emplaced across fields through which tanks could approach. Hills, clumps of woods, and groups of buildings outside the town might be defended as all-round strongpoints or at least combat outposts to deny or delay the enemy use of them or to prevent the town from being enveloped.

The main defence line was laid out in an irregular pattern to make it more difficult to locate, and prevent outflanking if penetrated. Particularly strong or dominating buildings were fortified as strongpoints on the main roads through the town. Snipers, anti-armour

Troops of the 85th Infantry Division search a fairly well-camouflaged German machine-gun position on Mt Altuzzo, Italy, in September 1944. A dugout is located at the position's right end. Two MG.42 machine guns were located in the position, providing a broad field of fire. Also in the position is a Torn.Fu.d2 radio indicating it may have doubled as an artillery observation post.

teams with *Panzerfausts*, and machine gunners were positioned in other buildings as well as placed forward of the main defence line along with small strongpoints. These disorganised the attackers before they reached the main defences. Secondary lines were prepared along with switch lines to contain penetrations. Even if a defended town was incorporated into a main defence line, it was prepared for all-round defence in case the external lines were penetrated and the town encircled. Reserves were positioned well inside the town in stout buildings while others might be held outside the town.

Streets could be blocked with roadblocks built of rubble, wrecked vehicles and streetcars, and heavy logs buried vertically. These log walls could be formidable obstacles up to 3–4m high and braced with angled logs, though these were more common in Germany. Rivers, streams and canals passing through towns were incorporated into the defence plan. Sometimes buildings were blown into streets blocking them with rubble. Mines were also used. Some streets were left unblocked to allow enemy tanks to move into close-range ambushes or tank-trapping cul-de-sacs. Side streets were sometimes blocked to prevent tanks from turning off when engaged. These roadblocks were recessed back into side streets to prevent their detection until passed. Town squares and traffic circles were set up as killing zones.

Buildings were booby-trapped and in some cases prepared with demolitions, to be detonated when the enemy occupied them. Doors and ground-floor windows were blocked with rubble and furniture, as were alleys. Other windows were left uncovered and open so that the enemy could not determine which windows were being fired from. Loopholes were knocked through walls and roof tiles and shingles removed. Many of these were unused, serving only to mislead the enemy. Positions were set up using chimneys for cover. Lookouts and artillery observers did use church belfries as posts, but once the enemy closed on the town they would evacuate them, as they were obvious targets. Snipers avoided them, despite what is often depicted in motion pictures. Attackers moved down streets hugging building walls. Defending riflemen and machine gunners took up positions on both sides of a street to cover the opposite side.

A log-reinforced dugout and rock-revetted fighting position on Mt Altuzzo, Italy, September 1944. This directed fire onto the forward slopes and across the La Rocca draw, which was an approach route. A camouflage net garnished with pine branches has been pulled away to reveal the position.

Residences were mostly constructed as adjoining rows of houses. 'Mouse-holes' (*Mauseloch*) were knocked through interior walls to connect the buildings on different floors including cellars. Doors sometimes connected the cellars of buildings on the same block. This allowed troops to reposition or reinforce. They were also used to reoccupy buildings that had been cleared by the enemy. Mouse-holes were sometimes concealed by furniture. Storm sewers were also used for movement between positions. Anti-armour and machine guns were positioned in cellars and other machine guns mounted in upper windows. Tanks had limited gun elevation and could not engage higher floor firing positions. Rubble piles had firing positions hidden in them. *Panzerfausts* were fired from alleys and other hidden sites in the open as they could not be fired from within buildings. Tanks and assault guns were concealed in buildings to fire down streets.

Ortona is on Italy's east-central coast opposite Rome and was the eastern anchor of the Gustav Line. The 10,000-population town was on level ground with the outskirts open, offering little cover. There were no natural terrain features to aid the defence. It had been hoped that the Germans would abandon the town and defend further north. The northern old town had narrow, twisting streets, large squares, and the buildings were more heavily constructed. The newer southern portion had wide straight streets. The buildings were stone and masonry with many 3–5 stories.

The Canadian Army experienced a tough fight on the southern approaches to Ortona. Two reinforced German paratrooper battalions defended the town covering a 500m x 1,500m area. The Germans defended in-depth using most of the tactics and techniques discussed previously. Intentionally blown-down buildings blocked most of the streets leaving only one main thoroughfare through the town's south-to-north axis, which chanelled the Canadian tanks into killing zones.

One extremely effective technique used to defend street intersections bounded by multi-storey buildings was to use demolitions to blow up the corner portions of the building on the enemy side. This exposed the interiors of the buildings across from the German-defended buildings. They might destroy a corner of one of their own buildings and use the rubble to barricade the street on the German side behind which were machine gunners and riflemen. They would withdraw when the attacker's fire became too intense. As the attackers crossed over the barricade machine guns sited in second- and third-storey windows further back down the street opened fire. An anti-armour gun might be positioned behind a barricade down the side street to engage any tanks that might approach the barricade as it crossed the street. Large demolition charges were emplaced in some buildings and command-detonated when occupied by the Canadians. Many houses were booby-trapped as were rubble piles used as cover by the attackers. Mines were hidden in barricades that tanks might try and crash through. In the north part of Ortona defence lines were established along the broad squares and separate buildings were demolished to deny cover to the attackers and provide wider fields of fire.

The Canadians launched their attack on 21 December 1943. The Germans were gradually pushed back through the town, falling back on successive strongpoints. Both defender's and attacker's tactics and techniques evolved through the battle with the Germans constantly introducing new methods. On the night of the 28th/29th the Germans withdrew after causing a nine-day delay to the Allied approach to the Gustav Line. Ortona was knicknamed 'Little Stalingrad' by the Canadians. They took over 2,300 casualties in Ortona plus larger numbers suffering from combat fatigue, and the 1st Canadian Division was temporarily combat ineffective.

Petsamo-Kirkenes, Finland, October 1944

The extreme north flank of the Eastern Front rested on the Barents Sea in an area where the borders of Norway, Finland and the USSR touched. In September 1944, after a major Soviet offensive mauled the Finnish Army (allied with Germany) in the south, Finland signed an armistice. It required that Finland expel or disarm German forces in the country, most of which were north of the Arctic Circle. The Germans soon began withdrawing to Norway. Units remained on the extreme north flank though to protect this withdrawal, as they could not move through Sweden. Not satisfied with the pace, the Soviets attacked in early October.

In the area of operations the north-eastward-flowing Titovka River defined the Finnish-Soviet border. German positions were as much as 12km inside the USSR on a strongpoint line (*Stutzpunktlinie*) known as the Litsa Front (after the river it was anchored on). The narrow coastal plain is covered with tundra and low rock hills with scores of rivers and streams flowing into the sea. Inland the terrain is barren, featuring rock hills and ridges up to 580m above sea level with scattered low brush and scrub trees. The many streams, ravines and gullies between the hills and ridges provide countless concealed avenues of approach. The waterlogged low ground cannot support vehicles and roads were few and crude. The Germans had occupied the area for three years and built a series of strongpoints in three belts. Only the first line was occupied. The second line was 10–12km west on the Titovka River while the third was another 20–25km west on the Petsamo River. These would be occupied as the Germans fell back.

The strongpoint lines were divided into battalion sectors (*Abschnitt*) with two reinforced company strongpoints and several platoon and half-platoon strongpoints with one or two interspaced between the company strongpoints. In the 2.Gebirgs-Division sector there were ten company strongpoints located atop hills. There was no depth to the strongpoint line, no mobile reserves and far too many concealed routes between strongpoints, the interval varying from 2–4km. These gaps were protected to some degree by patrols, obstacles, anti-personnel mines and indirect fire. When it became apparent that the Soviets would launch an offensive, a few additional positions were constructed and existing strongpoints improved. The Germans had only about one-third of the artillery the Soviets had, but they did have some air support.

The existing strongpoints were well built, being dug into rock. Some reinforced concrete positions had been built and most positions had heavy timber and rock overhead cover, the timber being brought from the south. Each strongpoint was self-contained with 360° fire and observation, and surrounded by barbed wire and mines. A serious problem was the rocky ground: it prevented the Germans from burying telephone lines, although it was run down trenches within strongpoints. Exposed wires would be cut by artillery and bomb fragments and command and control over the remote strongpoints would disintegrate. The Soviets had each strongpoint and its defences accurately plotted.

The strongpoints, manned by mountain troops, were usually oval in shape following the contour of their hilltop's crest. They were surrounded by single and double-apron barbed-wire fences with anti-personnel mines. Trenches connected all rifle and crew-served weapons position and support facilities. Each strongpoint was armed with light and heavy machine guns, 8cm mortars, 3.7cm anti-armour guns and 7.5cm infantry guns. Ammunition and ration stocks were abundant and all units were at about 90 per cent strength.

The Soviets attacked on 7 October with overwhelming artillery and air support. By the end of the second day Soviet troops had infiltrated the strongpoint line and were crossing the Titovka River in the south to isolate the strongpoints to the north and east of the river. Attacks were still being launched against the strongpoints. Late on the 8th the Germans were ordered to withdraw westward. Few of the strongpoints fell to direct assault and such attempts cost the Soviets heavily. With no in-depth positions or reserves, with communications often lost, the Germans were unable to hold out once the Soviets had infiltrated and got behind them. The strongpoint line was supposed to hold for 14 days allowing corps service units to withdraw, but they held out for less than three.

Palenberg, Germany, October 1944

As the First US Army approached the Third Reich's frontier in September 1944, its divisions readied themselves to fight a vicious battle to penetrate the much-vaunted Westwall. While beyond the scope of this book, the existing Westwall defences were incorporated into the German defence line, and are briefly examined here.

The 400km-long Westwall is often pictured as seemingly endless lines of concrete dragon's teeth anti-armour obstacles covered by countless massive reinforced concrete bunkers stretching the entire length of the German frontier. While posing a formidable obstacle, the Westwall was far from being continuous and as densely fortified as many feared. Defences were built in-depth from 2–20km, but were scattered in many areas and of uneven distribution. This depth is what gave the Allies the most difficulty, not the strength of the individual fortifications themselves. Largely built in the 1930s, by 1944 the positions were obsolete with most unable to mount anti-armour guns larger than 3.7cm. Many of the weapons on special mountings had been removed and employed in coast defences. Standard weapons could not always be mounted inside. The fields of fire were limited to 40–50° and could fire in only one direction, but were well-sited, covering key approaches. Casemated artillery positions were few in number and found covering only the most likely avenues of approach. The positions did have the tactical advantage of being over-grown with vegetation. Some additional work had been accomplished in the areas where attacks were most likely, especially in regards to additional anti-armour obstacles. Because of the limitations of the existing bunkers, coupled with the very real fear of being trapped in them, the Germans used them mostly as troop shelters and local command posts. They provided a central protected position around which field fortifications were dug. The bunkers were usually positioned in clusters of two tiers providing mutual support for adjacent bunkers. Trenches often linked bunkers within a cluster. Mutually supporting bunkers were usually 80–200m apart with second-tier bunkers 100–500m behind. There were gaps though between clusters of bunkers. The bunkers could be from less than 30m to up to 400m behind the anti-armour barrier (comprising anti-armour ditch, 4–6-row dragon's teeth, stone wall, steep-banked river, tank-proof dense woods, or railroad embankment). In sectors offering good infantry approaches from covered areas double-apron barbed wire was emplaced using steel picket posts. The Germans did an excellent job of tying the defences into natural terrain obstacles to limit the number of man-made obstacles built.

While there were many types of concrete fortications employed on the Westwall, those covering the defence zone usually contained a 3.7cm gun (mostly removed with a machine gun substituted) plus a machine gun or just a single machine gun in the battle room, one or two rooms for troop quarters, ammunition room, storage locker, and a gas-proof vestibule with one or two entrances. Most had an emergency exit. Walls were 2m thick and the roofs 2.5m. They were semi-sunken with most of the above-ground portion covered by sodded-over earth. They sometimes had a building façade built around them for camouflage. Tunnels did not connect them. Telephone cables buried up to 2m deep connected all positions and command posts. They contained folding bunks, lights (though generators had often been removed), tables, benches, wall-mounted telephones, stoves and gas filter systems. Five to seven men manned most. Three were on watch with the remainder inside resting. When shelled all sought cover inside. When attacked all but the machine gunners left the bunker and occupied field works. The doors were often unprotected from direct fire by exterior blast walls or trenches. A tank or bazooka round could penetrate the steel doors.

Strongpoints were prepared around bunkers or bunker clusters and small clumps of woods. These consisted of L-, V- and W-shaped rifle, machine-gun, and *Panzerfaust/Panzerschreck* positions covering all approaches. Some positions were dispersed along roads leading into the strongpoints and the roads were mined with many being booby-trapped. Anti-armour ditches were sometimes defended with firing steps and dugouts cut in their sides. Mortar positions were located to the rear to cover the approaches to the strongpoints and gaps between clusters. In areas where the risk of attack had originally been deemed slight there were fewer permanent fortifications and field works were denser.

To provide an 'ideal' model of what the permanent fortifications entailed, a 3km section of the Westwall at Palenberg, a small coal mining town 13.5km north of Aachen, defended by the 49.Infantrie-Division, is examined here – the point where the 30th US Infantry Division attacked. The terrain was gently rolling, mostly open ground. The scattered narrow bands of woods were incorporated into the anti-armour barriers. The Wurm River ran in front of the defences, but while

Table 3: defences of Palenberg, Germany
1,500m anti-armour ditch
600m anti-armour ditch with a 700m ditch 600–800m behind it
1,500 and 600m sections were tied into railroad embankment
30 machine-gun bunkers (6 forward of anti-armour barrier)
8 machine-gun bunkers in second-line cluster north of Palenberg
5 troop bunkers (3 forward of anti-armour barrier)
1 open position with 3 x 2cm flak guns

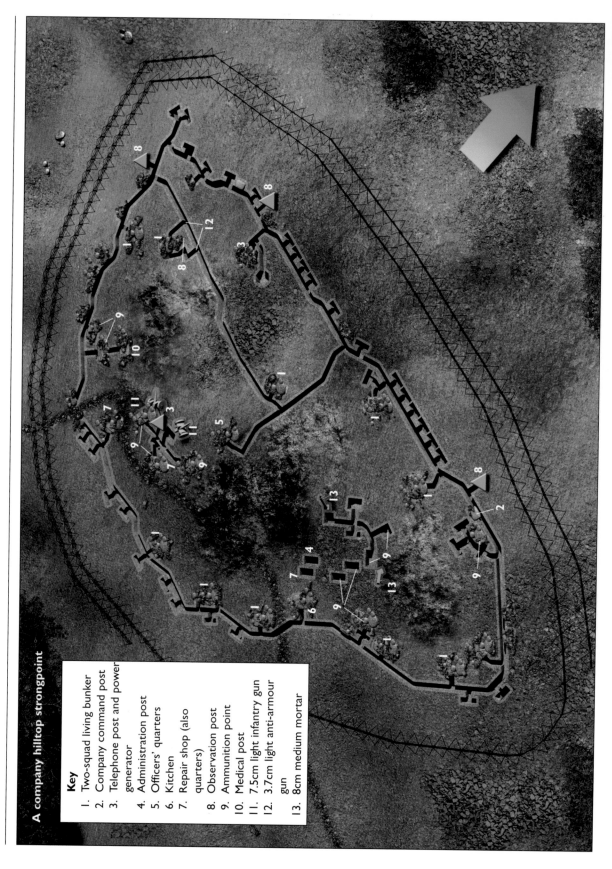

A company hilltop strongpoint

Key

1. Two-squad living bunker
2. Company command post
3. Telephone post and power generator
4. Administration post
5. Officers' quarters
6. Kitchen
7. Repair shop (also quarters)
8. Observation post
9. Ammunition point
10. Medical post
11. 7.5cm light infantry gun
12. 3.7cm light anti-armour gun
13. 8cm medium mortar

A company hilltop strongpoint

Stutzpunkt Zuckerhutl was typical of the company strongpoints in the far north of Finland in 1944. It was surrounded by two parallel double-apron barbed-wire fences with anti-personnel mines. A firing trench revetted with rock and mortar ran around the entire perimeter with communications trenches connected to support positions in the centre. The defenders were a 1st Mountain Infantry Regiment, 2nd Mountain Division rifle company reinforced with a pioneer platoon, crew-served weapons from the battalion, and artillery forward observers. They were armed with 13 light and 8 heavy machine guns, two 8cm mortars, two 3.7cm anti-armour guns and two 7.5cm infantry guns, the normal allocation of weapons from the battalion heavy companies and the regimental anti-armour company. Two-man firing positions and machine-gun bunkers lined the perimeter. The reason for the apparently irregular spacing of these positions is their siting to cover the approaches across broken terrain. Troops were quartered in various support bunkers and two-squad bunkers. Note that the command post is on the forward perimeter enabling the commander to directly observe the enemy. The large red arrow indicates the direction towards the enemy (*feindwärts*).

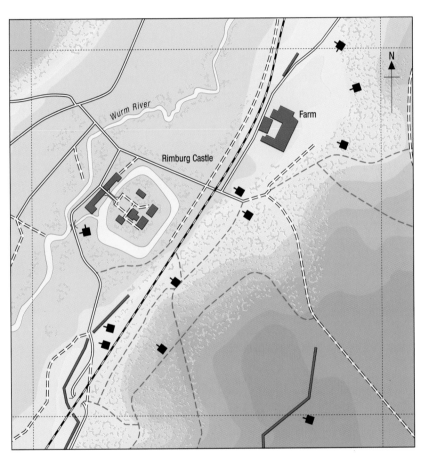

LEFT Westwall defences, Germany, October 1944. The 1,100m² area shown lies immediately to the south of Palenberg. The moated Rimburg Castle, to the centre left, was heavily defended, as was the large farm complex to the upper right of the castle. The Wurm River flows through the upper left area – itself an obstacle with its bridges blown. The double railroad tracks were on an elevated embankment, which was incorporated into the defences to form an anti-armour obstacle. Where the embankment is low an anti-armour ditch was built (the heavy grey line in the lower left). The end of a second-line anti-armour ditch is visible in the lower right corner. Ten concrete bunkers within this square covered the railroad embankment and anti-armour ditch, and a further one is shown covering the second-line anti-armour ditch. Some six or so rifle, machine-gun and *Panzerschreck* positions were dug around these bunkers, with some of them connected by trenches.

only 10m wide, its steep banks and marshy adjacent ground provided an excellent tank obstacle. All bridges had been blown. A steep-sided double railroad track embankment traversed the width of this sector running parallel with the Wurm and was tied into anti-armour ditches. There were no dragon's teeth in this sector. The bunkers were by no means evenly distributed across the front, but sited to cover the most likely avenues of approach. Grenadier and machine-gun battalions defended the sector backed by significant artillery with some armour in reserve.

The US 30th Infantry Division attacked in this sector on 2 October after conducting extensive rehearsals and weapons training. Casualties were heavy the first day with many sustained by intense artillery and mortar fire. A foothold was secured within the defences even though supporting tanks experienced difficulties crossing the Wurm. Heavy machine-gun fire was

The defences of a German town annotated by US aerial photo interpreters. Warehouses are located on the left edge above a railway yard. A row of houses stretches to the right of the warehouses and more dwellings can be seen in the lower right. The continuous, barbed-wire protected, first-line trench stretches across the photo's top with machine guns positioned in pairs. A position containing three 2cm Flak guns is in the upper right. Communications trenches run to the rear: these also served as flanking-fire trenches in the event of an Allied penetration of the first line. The second trench line covers the anti-tank ditch and it was from here that counter-attacks would be launched. The anti-tank ditch is linked to the row of houses and the warehouses, which probably have strongpoints located within some of the buildings. There were also probably mines and anti-armour obstacles blocking passages between buildings. Oddly, mortar positions are located forward of the second line.

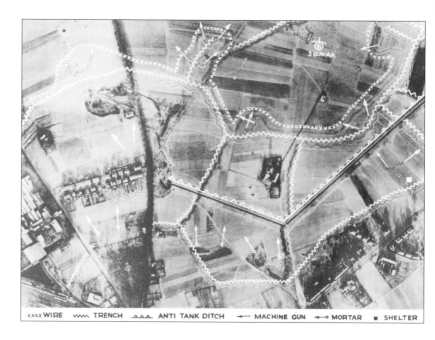

xxxx WIRE   ᴍᴍ TRENCH   ▴▴▴ ANTI TANK DITCH   ←— MACHINE GUN   ←○ MORTAR   ▪ SHELTER

This hastily built MG.34 position in Germany possesses a good field of fire, but is poorly camouflaged because of the exposed spoil around its forward parapet.

directed on the bunker firing ports while mortars and machine guns suppressed adjacent field works. Three or four tanks or tank destroyers supported a rifle platoon attacking a bunker with bazookas, satchel and pole charges, and flamethrowers. Often the latter had only to fire a burst into the air and the Germans surrendered. 105mm self-propelled howitzers were especially useful for engaging bunkers. Most bunkers were blown once seized up using 1,200lbs (544kg) of TNT to prevent their recapture and use.

The Germans counter-attacked that night supported by armour, but failed to dislodge the Americans. German morale was initially high, but once the main defence zone was penetrated their morale began to suffer. The defences had been completely penetrated in the 30th Infantry Division's sector by 6 October. At that time the division swung south and began rolling up the flank and rear of the Westwall defences rather than continuing to advance eastward as the Germans expected. This unanticipated move caused German morale to rapidly crumble. By 16 October the division had cleared an area 12km south to the outskirts of Aachen from its original penetration of the Westwall and linked up with the 1st Infantry Division. The division had suffered 2,030 casualties, fewer than forecast, and created a 13km-wide breech into Germany. The Americans evaluated that the permanent fortifications, though extensive, only enhanced the German defence by 15 per cent over defences comprising field works only. Dug-in German tanks and assault guns were given an efficiency rating of 40 per cent and considered much more troublesome than bunkers.

An assessment of German field fortifications

German field fortifications were highly developed and were as effective as any others employed during the war. The specified designs of individual positions were well thought out, and were designed to protect against direct and indirect fire and from being overrun by tanks. They could accommodate troops and weapons, allowing them to take full advantage of their capabilities. However, individual positions, no matter how well designed, were ineffective unless fully integrated into a defensive system that coordinated the various elements of adjacent positions, obstacles, fire support, reserves and command and control. Avenues of approach and obstacles (including minefields) needed to be kept under constant observation to prevent surprise attacks. Camouflage and concealment from both ground and air observation were essential, including deception measures such as decoys and dummy positions. The overall layout and layering of the defences in depth was also essential to a successful defence. German troops were capable of achieving all of this, and often did so (with time, resources, weather and the tactical and operational situations permitting).

In most instances the Germans, at all levels, adhered to the basic precepts of selecting, locating and building field fortifications. For the most part they were well positioned, effectively covered their assigned sectors of observation and fire, provided mutual support to adjacent positions, made good use of their weapon's capabilities, were well camouflaged (especially at ground level), and fitted well within the terrain and avenues of approach to their positions. In particular, the obstacles employed made good use of natural features to create more effective barriers, but there were many instances when the Germans failed to maintain observation and fire on these areas – more a result of a specific tactical situation or a lack of resources as opposed to the neglecting of key principles. Camouflage was sometimes deficient, especially overhead, a factor usually due to insufficient time and resources, coupled with the inherent difficulties of hiding from airborne observation.

The Germans demonstrated a great deal of flexibility, ingenuity and initiative in adapting their doctrinal defensive tactics and techniques to the varying terrain and weather conditions on different fronts. Field fortifications and obstacles were modified and new ones designed to exploit locally available materials (vital when considering how limited supplies were) as well as to attempt to counter new Allied assault tactics and heavier armour.

Regardless of the front on which the Germans defended, the most significant problem they faced was the lack of sufficient troops to provide adequate in-depth defence, and of armour and other motorised units for a mobile reserve allowing rapid and hard-hitting counter-attacks. No defence could resist a strong, well-coordinated, combined-arms

While mud could severely hinder offensive operations, it also made life difficult for defenders dug into field fortifications.

The well-built, multi-storey, interconnected buildings of European urban areas provided robust defensive positions. When destroyed, the rubble created countless hiding places for defenders and obstacles to the attackers.

attack supported by massive artillery and air resources. The defence line could be restored or partly restored if strong mobile reserves could conduct substantial counter-attacks, but the lack of air defence cover, or rather the air superiority of the Allies, prevented the timely commitment of mobile reserves even when they were available.

The Allies developed extremely effective offensive tactics to deal with German defences. Allied basic doctrine was repeatedly modified and perfected as new weapons came available and lessons were learned. No two units, even within the same division, used the same assault tactics.

German combat troops in particular realised the fallacy of fixed, permanent defences, such as on the Westwall: these were used to strengthen the field fortifications, and not vice versa. Ultimately, the Germans were rarely able to develop complete mobile or elastic defences as specified by doctrine. What the defences did do was buy time at a strategic level. It should be noted that it took the Soviets from February 1943 (after the fall of Stalingrad) until 30 April 1945 (the fall of Berlin) – some 27 months – to bring the Germans to the point of defeat.

Little remains today of these field fortifications. In most areas new construction, agriculture and government polices have covered over the mostly temporary sites. Many of the semi-permanent concrete fortifications have been demolished too. However, in some remote areas of Germany, France, the former USSR and other countries, traces of trench lines and shallow, overgrown depressions can be found, marking the vanished frontiers of the Third Reich.

Bibliography

Fleischer, Wolfgang *Feldbefestigungen des deutschen Heeres, 1939–1945* (Podzum-Pallas Verlag, Wölersheim-Berstadt, 1998). A reprint of a 1944 German field fortifications manual with additional background and introductory material added. The text is in German.

German Field Works of World War II (Bellona Publications Ltd., Bracknell, Berkshire, 1969). This is a reprint of a 1942 German field fortifications manual. It contains German text with annotations in English.

Kaufmann, J.E. and Kuffmann, H.W. *Fortress Third Reich: German Fortifications and Defence Systems in World War II* (Da Capo Press, Cambridge, MA, 2003).

War Department (US Army) *Handbook on German Military Forces*, TM E-30-451, 15 March 1945. Several reprints have been published in past years.

Wray, Timothy A. *Standing Fast: German Defensive Doctrine on the Russian Front During World War II: pre-war to March 1943*. Research Survey No. 5 (Combat Studies Institute, Ft Leavenworth, KS, 1986).

Glossary

Abwehr defence
AFV armoured fighting vehicle (tanks, assault guns, halftracks, armoured cars, reconnaissance vehicles)
Beobachtrungsposten/stand observation post
In deckung under cover (overhead cover)
Deutschen Heer German Army
Feindwärts direction towards the enemy
Feldhaubitze (F.H.) field howitzer
Feuerstellung firing position (crew-served weapons)
Fliegerabwehrkanone (Flak) air-defence gun
Führungstelle command post
Geschutzestellung gun emplacement
Graben trench
Granatwerfer (Gr.W.) mortar
Hindernis obstacle
Infanterie Geschütz (iG.) infantry gun
In Felsen gehauene rock-encased position (sangar)
Leicht (le.) light (weapon)
Luftschutzraum air-raid shelter

Mashinengewehr (MG.) machine gun
Mine, Minensperre mine, minefield
Munitionslöchern ammunition niche
NCO non-commissioned officer
Nest nest (mortar or gun position, obsolete 1943)
Panzerabwehrkanone (Pak.) anti-armour gun
Panzerdeckungslöchern armour protection hole/trench
Posten post (guard post, outpost)
Schussfeld field of fire
Schwer (s.) heavy (weapon)
Sicherungposten security outpost
Stapelplatz dump (ammunition, supply)
Stellung/stand station, position
Toter raum dead ground/space
Unterschlupfe dugout
Unterstand bunker
Vorposten outpost
Wagenpark vehicle park
Wirkungsbereich field of fire

Index

OSPREY
PUBLISHING

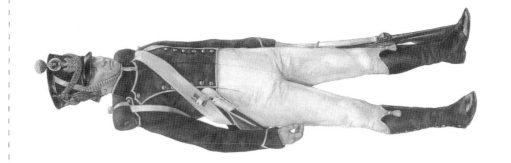

FIND OUT MORE ABOUT OSPREY

❏ Please send me the latest listing of Osprey's publications

❏ I would like to subscribe to Osprey's e-mail newsletter

Title / rank

Name

Address

City / county

Postcode / zip   state / country

e-mail

FOR

I am interested in:

❏ Ancient world
❏ Medieval world
❏ 16th century
❏ 17th century
❏ 18th century
❏ Napoleonic
❏ 19th century

❏ American Civil War
❏ World War 1
❏ World War 2
❏ Modern warfare
❏ Military aviation
❏ Naval warfare

Please send to:

USA & Canada:
Osprey Direct USA, c/o MBI Publishing, P.O. Box 1, 729 Prospect Avenue, Osceola, WI 54020

UK, Europe and rest of world:
Osprey Direct UK, P.O. Box 140, Wellingborough, Northants, NN8 2FA, United Kingdom

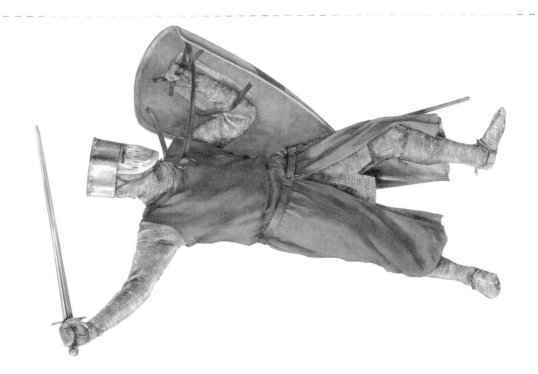

OSPREY
PUBLISHING

www.ospreypublishing.com

call our telephone hotline
for a free information pack

USA & Canada: 1-800-826-6600
UK, Europe and rest of world call:
+44 (0) 1933 443 863

Young Guardsman
Figure taken from *Warrior 22:*
Imperial Guardsman 1799–1815
Published by Osprey
Illustrated by Richard Hook

Knight, c.1190
Figure taken from *Warrior 1: Norman Knight 950 – 1204 AD*
Published by Osprey
Illustrated by Christa Hook

POSTCARD